Past Masters
General Editor   Keith Thomas

Jung

Anthony Stevens is a distinguished Jungian analyst,
psychiatrist, and writer on Jungian themes. He is a
graduate of Oxford University and in addition to his
DM has two degrees in psychology. His previous
books include *Archetype: A Natural History of the
Self* (1982), *The Roots of War* (1989), *On Jung* (1990),
and *The Two Million-Year-Old Self* (1993).

Past Masters

AQUINAS Anthony Kenny
ARISTOTLE Jonathan Barnes
ARNOLD Stefan Collini
AUGUSTINE Henry Chadwick
BACH Denis Arnold
FRANCIS BACON Anthony Quinton
BAYLE Elisabeth Labrousse
BENTHAM John Dinwiddy
BERKELEY J. O. Urmson
THE BUDDHA Michael Carrithers
BURKE C. B. Macpherson
CERVANTES P. E. Russell
CLAUSEWITZ Michael Howard
COBBETT Raymond Williams
COLERIDGE Richard Holmes
DARWIN Jonathan Howard
DESCARTES Tom Sorell
DIDEROT Peter France
DISRAELI John Vincent
DURKHEIM Frank Parkin
GEORGE ELIOT Rosemary Ashton
ENGELS Terrell Carver
ERASMUS James McConica
FREUD Anthony Storr
GALILEO Stillman Drake
GIBBON J. W. Burrow
GOETHE T. J. Reed
HEGEL Peter Singer
HOBBES Richard Tuck
HOMER Jasper Griffin
HUME A. J. Ayer
JESUS Humphrey Carpenter

JOHNSON Pat Rogers
JUNG Anthony Stevens
KANT Roger Scruton
KIERKEGAARD Patrick Gardiner
LAMARCK L. J. Jordanova
LEIBNIZ G. MacDonald Ross
LOCKE John Dunn
MACHIAVELLI Quentin Skinner
MALTHUS Donald Winch
MARX Peter Singer
MENDEL Vitezslav Orel
MONTAIGNE Peter Burke
MONTESQUIEU Judith N. Shklar
THOMAS MORE Anthony Kenny
WILLIAM MORRIS Peter Stansky
MUHAMMAD Michael Cook
NEWMAN Owen Chadwick
PAINE Mark Philp
PAUL E. P. Sanders
PLATO R. M. Hare
PROUST Derwent May
RUSKIN George P. Landow
SCHILLER T. J. Reed
SHAKESPEARE Germaine Greer
ADAM SMITH D. D. Raphael
SPINOZA Roger Scruton
TOCQUEVILLE Larry Siedentop
VICO Peter Burke
VIRGIL Jasper Griffin
WITTGENSTEIN A. C. Grayling
WYCLIF Anthony Kenny

Forthcoming

JOSEPH BUTLER R. G. Frey
COPERNICUS Owen Gingerich
GODWIN Alan Ryan
KEYNES Robert Skidelsky
NIETZSCHE Michael Tanner

ROUSSEAU Robert Wokler
RUSSELL A. C. Grayling
SCHOPENHAUER Christopher
    Janaway
and others

Anthony Stevens

Jung

Oxford   New York

OXFORD UNIVERSITY PRESS

1994

Oxford University Press, Walton Street, Oxford OX2 6DP

Oxford New York Toronto
Delhi Bombay Calcutta Madras Karachi
Kuala Lumpur Singapore Hong Kong Tokyo
Nairobi Dar es Salaam Cape Town
Melbourne Auckland Madrid
and associated companies in
Berlin Ibadan

150.1954
St47j

Oxford is a trade mark of Oxford University Press

First published 1994 as an Oxford University Press paperback

British Library Cataloguing in Publication Data
Data available

Library of Congress Cataloging in Publication Data
Stevens, Anthony.
Jung/Anthony Stevens.
p.   cm.—(Past masters)
Includes bibliographical references and index.
1. Jung, C. G. (Carl Gustav), 1875–1961.   2. Psychoanalysis.
3. Psychoanalysts—Austria—Biography.   I. Title.   II. Series.
[DNLM: 1. Jung, C. G. (Carl Gustav), 1875–1961.   2. Jungian
Theory.   WM 460]
BF109.J8S74   1994
for Library of Congress   150.19'54—dc20   93–23096
ISBN 0–19–287686–4

10 9 8 7 6 5 4 3 2 1

Typeset by Best-Set Typesetter Ltd., Hong Kong
Printed in Great Britain by
Biddles Ltd
Guildford and King's Lynn

To Chuck and Sue Schwartz

Preface

To give a comprehensive account of Jung and his Psychology (commonly referred to as *analytical psychology* to distinguish it from Freud's *psychoanalysis* and from *experimental psychology*, the pure science of the academics) in a slim volume of 128 pages is a tall order. Jung was both a polymath and prolific writer: in addition to psychology, psychiatry, and medicine, he had an encyclopaedic knowledge of mythology, religion, philosophy, gnosticism, and alchemy, knew English, French, Latin, and Greek, as well as his native German, and was at home in the literature of each. Although he carried this massive erudition with a cheerful lack of pomposity, it is evident in everything he wrote; and since he was not good at organizing his material, *The Collected Works of C. G. Jung* in twenty large volumes afford a daunting prospect to the uninitiated reader.

Jung recognized his failings as a communicator ('Nobody reads my books', he said, and 'I have such a hell of a trouble to make people see what I mean'), but this awareness did not prompt him to revise his work in the same systematic way as Freud. Consequently, much time and labour are required to understand Jung from his original papers and books, and while there can be no escape from the effort involved if one wishes to stake one's claim to a portion of Jung's rich legacy, the task can be made less arduous by a concise introduction of the type this small book is meant to provide.

Acknowledgements

I should like to express my thanks to Routledge and the Princeton University Press for permission to quote from *The Collected Works of C. G. Jung*; to Random House, Inc. for permission to quote from *Memories, Dreams, Reflections* by C. G. Jung, recorded and edited by Aniela Jaffé; and to Routledge for permission to reproduce the diagram on p. 34 from *On Jung*.

I must also thank my secretary, Norma Luscombe, for word processing the original manuscript with infinite care and goodwill, and Mary Worthingon for her skilful editing of the final product.

Contents

1 The man and his psychology

Jung was a man of paradox. In one sense he was an individualist, a great eccentric. In another he was the living embodiment of the universal man. He strove to realize in his own life his full human potential; but he was determined, at the same time, to live in an uncompromisingly unique way. If this meant upsetting people, as was often the case, he did not, on the whole, seem to mind. 'To be normal', he said, 'is the ideal aim of the unsuccessful.'

Although considering himself a rational scientist, he was willing to give his attention to matters conventionally regarded as irrational or esoteric, and he was not unduly perturbed on those occasions when such interests put him beyond the scientific pale. In his view, to adopt an exclusively rational attitude to human psychology was not only inadequate but, in the light of history, preposterous. He had to keep faith with the truth as he saw it, and it was not his fault if this led him into realms of theory and experience which were deeply at variance with the prejudices and preoccupations of his time. 'I feel it is the duty of one who goes his own way to inform society of what he finds on his voyage of discovery,' he wrote.

Not the criticism of individual contemporaries will decide the truth or falsity of these discoveries, but future generations. There are things that are not yet true today, perhaps we dare not find them true, but tomorrow they may be. So every man whose fate it is to go his individual way must proceed with hopefulness and watchfulness, ever conscious of his loneliness and its dangers. (CW VII, para. 201)

This sense of being drawn by destiny to swim against the prevailing tide makes him a richly intriguing character. And it means that any book on Jungian psychology has to take full account of the life and personality of its founder, for, more than any other psychologist, Jung's understanding of humanity grew directly out of his understanding of himself.

Throughout his long life, Jung remained a deeply introverted man, more interested in the inner world of dreams and images than

1

in the outer world of people and events. From childhood he possessed a genius for introspection which enabled him to attend closely to experiences proceeding on or below the threshold of consciousness—experiences of which the great majority of us remain almost completely unaware. This gift was derived, at least in part, from the peculiar circumstances of his birth and upbringing.

Background

Born in the hamlet of Kesswil on the Swiss shore of Lake Constance on 26 July 1875, Jung was the only son of the village pastor, the Reverend Paul Achilles Jung and Emilie Jung, née Preiswerk. His grandfather, Carl Gustav Jung (1794–1864), after whom he was christened, was a much respected physician, who became Rector of Basel University and Grand Master of the Swiss Lodge of Freemasons. He was rumoured to be the illegitimate son of Goethe. Though he bore a strong physical resemblance to the great poet, this is probably a legend and not fact.

Jung's mother was the youngest daughter of Samuel Preiswerk (1799–1871), a well-known but eccentric theologian, who devoted his life to studying Hebrew in the belief that it was the language spoken in heaven. He was an early advocate of Zionism, had visions, and held conversations with the dead. Right up to the time of her marriage, Emilie was obliged to sit behind him as he composed his sermons in order to stop the devil peering over his shoulder. Most male members of the large Preiswerk family were clergymen, who shared Samuel's preoccupation with the occult. This Jung–Preiswerk mixture of medicine, theology, and spiritualism was to have its influence on Carl's intellectual development.

The family moved twice during Jung's childhood, first to Laufen, near the Falls of the Rhine, when he was six months old, and then to Klein-Hüningen, just outside Basel, when he was four. Neither of the large vicarages which they inhabited provided a happy environment for a growing child. In his autobiography, *Memories, Dreams, Reflections*, Jung describes the home atmosphere as 'unbreathable': he says he was oppressed with a pervasive sense of death, melancholy, and unease, and with 'dim intimations of trouble' between his parents. He tells us that they did not share the same bedroom and that he, Carl, slept with his father. When he was 3, his mother had a breakdown for which she had to spend several months in hospital, and this enforced separation at a critical stage in his development seems to have affected Jung for the rest of his life. This is not an unlikely consequence, for, as has been well established by John Bowlby and his followers, the despair displayed by young children on loss of their mother is a normal response to frustration of their absolute need for her presence. Should this disaster occur, children usually manage to survive, it is true, but at the cost of developing a defensive attitude of emotional detachment, and by becoming self-absorbed and self-reliant to an unusual degree. Typically, they are left with lasting doubts about their capacity to elicit care and affection. They also tend to become odd and aloof in manner, which does not endear them to others. Although Carl was cared for by an aunt and a maid while his mother was away, he recalled being 'deeply troubled' by her absence: he suffered from nervous eczema and had terrifying dreams. 'From then on,' he says, 'I always felt mistrustful when the word "love" was spoken. The feeling I associated with "woman" was for a long time that of innate unreliability' (*MDR* 23).

Jung's father was a kind, tolerant man, but his son experienced him as powerless, and emotionally immature. Quite early in his ministry, Paul Jung seems to have lost his faith, but, lacking any alternative source of income, felt compelled to persevere with his parish duties. The strain of keeping up the appearance of piety while lacking all religious conviction helped to turn him into a querulous hypochondriac whom it was difficult for his wife and son to love or respect.

An only child until his sister Gertrud was born in 1884, Carl was unhappy at school, feeling alienated both from his companions and from his inner self: his rather schizoid (i.e. withdrawn, aloof, and self-absorbed) manner made him unpopular, and the school environment was one in which he just could not flourish. A sense of personal singularity was aggravated by traumatic incidents, as when a master accused him of plagiarizing an essay which he had composed with immense care. When he protested his innocence, his schoolmates sided with the master. Such experiences made him feel 'branded' and utterly alone. For a long period he dropped out altogether, having developed a proneness to fainting attacks after a blow on the head when knocked over by another boy. (As he lay on the ground, much longer than necessary, he thought to himself, 'Now you won't have to go to school any more.') He spent as much time as he could on his own. 'I remained alone with my thoughts. On the whole I liked that best. I played alone, day-dreamed or strolled in the woods alone, and had a secret world of my own' (*MDR* 58).

This secret world compensated for his isolation. The fantasies and rituals common to childhood assumed a heightened intensity for him, and they influenced the rest of his life. For example, his adult delight in studying alone in a tower he built for himself at Bollingen on the upper lake of Zürich was anticipated by a childhood ritual in which he kept a carved manikin in a pencil box hidden away on a beam in the vicarage attic. From time to time, he visited the manikin and presented him with scrolls written in a secret language to provide him with a library in the fastness of his attic retreat. This gave Carl a feeling of 'newly won security' which sustained him through his father's irritable moods, his mother's depressive invalidism, and his 'alienation' at school. 'No one could discover my secret and destroy it. I felt safe, and the tormenting sense of being at odds with myself was gone' (*MDR* 34).

Another childhood ritual prepared him for his later insights into the importance of *projection* in psychology. It was an imaginative game which he played as he sat on a large stone in the garden. He would intone, 'I am sitting on top of this stone and it is under-neath.' Immediately, the stone would reply, 'I am lying here on this slope and he is sitting on top of me.' Then he would ask himself, 'Am I the one who is sitting on the stone, or am I the stone on which *he* is sitting?' This left him with 'a feeling of curious and fascinating darkness', but he knew that his secret relationship with the stone held some unfathomable significance (*MDR* 33). In this game we can trace the origins of Jung's mature insight into the mysteries of alchemy—that the alchemists had *projected* the contents of their own psyches into the materials on which they worked in their laboratories.

Jung's adult delight in solitude, his alchemical studies, and his research into the dynamics of psychic transformation were also foreshadowed in an adolescent fantasy which entertained him as he walked each day from the vicarage at Klein-Hüningen to the school he attended in Basel. It was a vision of an ideal world in which everything would be better than it was. There would be no school and life could be arranged exactly as he wished. On a rock rising out of a lake sat a well-fortified castle with a tall keep, a watchtower, surrounded by a small medieval city, ruled by a council of elders. The castle was Carl's home. Here he lived as Justice of the Peace, emerging only occasionally 'to hold court'. In the harbour lay his personal two-masted schooner, armed with an array of small cannon.

The crux of the fantasy was the keep: it contained a wonderful secret of which Carl was the sole possessor. Inside the tower, extending from the battlements down to the vaulted cellar, was a copper column as thick as a man's arm: at the top were fine branches or filaments extending into the air. These extracted a 'spiritual essence' from the atmosphere which the copper column drew down into the cellar, where there was a laboratory in which he transformed the airy substance into gold. 'This was certainly no mere conjuring trick, but a venerable and vitally important secret of nature which had come to me I know not how and which I had to conceal not only from the council of elders but, in a sense, also from myself' (*MDR* 87).

The need to create a citadel in which to hide from the world is characteristic of people with a schizoid disposition. Young Carl's castle was defensively fortified and only tenuously connected to the mainland by a narrow isthmus cut through by a broad canal, with a drawbridge over it. Later, he began building model castles, surrounded by fortified emplacements, and he spent hours studying the virtually impregnable fortifications of Vauban.

Within the security of his inner citadel, Carl experienced himself as made up of two separate personalities, which he referred to as 'No. 1' and 'No. 2' respectively. No. 1 was the son of his parents who went to school and coped with life as well as he could, while No. 2 was much older, remote from the world of human society, but close to nature and animals, to dreams, and to God. He conceived No. 2 as 'having no definable character at all—born, living, dead, everything in one, a total vision of life' (*MDR* 92). As a psychiatrist he came to understand that these two personalities were not unique to himself but present in everyone. However, he acknowledged that he was apparently more aware of them than most, particularly of No. 2. 'In my life No. 2 has been of prime importance, and I have always tried to make room for anything that wanted to come from within' (*MDR* 55). Much later he was to rename these two personalities the ego and the Self and to maintain that the play and counter-play between them constitutes the central dynamic of personality development.

He believed that his No. 2 personality conferred on him a privilege denied to his unfortunate father, namely, direct access to the mind of God. This was confirmed for him by the revelatory nature of his dreams, which contained images (such as that of an underground phallic deity which occurred when he was only 3) which he knew must derive from a source beyond himself, and by a powerful vision, which he struggled unsuccessfully to resist, of the Almighty seated on a golden throne defecating on the roof of Basel Cathedral (which signified to him, not unreasonably, that God had scant respect for His Church). Such revelations made him intolerant of his father's spiritual perplexity and gave rise to heated discussions between them. Whenever Carl tackled him with religious questions the pastor became irritable and defensive: 'You always want to *think*,' he complained. 'One ought not to think, but *believe*.' The boy reflected inwardly, 'No, one must experience and *know*!' But aloud he said, 'Give me this belief.' Whereupon his father merely shrugged and turned away.

Matters came to a head with Carl's confirmation, for which his father prepared him. He reached the pinnacle of religious initiation and was appalled to find that he experienced nothing whatsoever. An unbridgeable gulf opened between him and his father, for whom he felt 'a most vehement pity'. 'All at once I understood the tragedy of his profession and his life . . . I saw how hopelessly he was entrapped by the Church and its theological teaching . . . I now found myself cut off by the Church and from my father's and everybody else's faith' (*MDR* 64–5).

Whereas other boys in similar circumstances might have turned to their peers for support, Carl Jung, possessing no friends, turned inwards to embrace his 'No. 2', the Self. Throughout his adolescence he experienced the Self as God-like and the strength of his commitment to this internal 'other' took precedence over all outer relationships. He did not feel himself to be among people, but alone with God.

Inevitably, this confirmed him not in the Church but in his isolation: 'Other people all seemed to have totally different concerns. I felt completely alone with my certainties. More than ever I wanted someone to talk to, but nowhere did I find a point of contact . . . Why has no one had similar experiences to mine? I wondered . . . Why should I be the only one?' (*MDR* 71).

He cured himself of his fainting attacks when one day he overheard his father telling an acquaintance about his grave anxiety for his son's future. He returned to school and applied himself to his studies. Lacking all communication with like minds, he turned to literature, philosophy, and the history of religion. Heraclitus was to prove a lifelong favourite, as were Goethe and Meister Eckhart. He was much excited by Schopenhauer's *The World as Will and Idea*, which, together with Kant's *Critique of Pure Reason*, brought him such illumination that, he says, it revolutionized his attitude to the world and to life. In Goethe's *Faust* he found a legendary equivalent of his own No. 2 personality and this not only heightened his feeling of inner security but gave him, rather belatedly, a 'sense of belonging to the human community' (*MDR* 93).

Student years

Jung enrolled as a student at Basel University in 1895. It is characteristic of him that his decision to study natural science and medicine was determined not so much by his reading as by his dreams. Student life seems to have had a liberating effect on him, as did the premature death of his father at the age of 54, when Jung was only 21. ('He died in time for you,' his mother commented darkly.) 'I now began to display a tremendous appetite on all fronts. I knew what I wanted and went after it. I also became noticeably more accessible and communicative' (*MDR* 93).

One idea that Jung borrowed from Heraclitus was to be of crucial importance to him: the notion that all entities possess an inherent tendency to turn into their opposite. This tendency Heraclitus called *enantiodromia* (lit. 'running counter to'). Jung believed it to be characteristic of all dynamic systems, and saw the human family as a prime example: as children grow up, they display a propensity to compensate in their own lives for the failings of their parents. This tendency was particularly apparent in Jung himself, and his life may be understood in many ways as an effort to make good his father's deficiencies.

Whereas Paul Jung was spiritually timid, intellectually incurious, and inclined to accept dogma, showed signs of emotional immaturity, and ducked the major issues of his life, Carl, by contrast, was to display spiritual courage and intellectual rigour, resisted dogma wherever he encountered it, spent his life refining techniques for the development of the personality, and was disposed to confront all important issues head on, even when this meant courting unpopularity or disapproval.

The same compensatory propensity turned him into a lifelong gnostic (Greek, *gnostikos*, one who knows)—one dedicated to knowing the reality of the psyche through direct experience and personal revelation. It was this quest for gnosis which led him to grant fundamental importance to his dreams, fantasies, and visions, to attempt to understand them through the study of literature, philosophy, and religion, and, ultimately, to adopt psychiatry as a career.

A crucial dream came shortly after he commenced his studies at Basel. He dreamt that it was night-time and he was making painful headway through dense fog against a mighty wind, his hands cupped round a tiny light, which threatened to go out at any moment. Feeling there was something behind him, he glanced backwards and saw that he was being followed by a gigantic black figure. He was terrified, but knew he would be all right as long as he could keep his little light flickering through the murky night and the wind. 'When I awoke,' he says, 'I realized at once that the figure was a "spectre of the Brocken", my own shadow on the swirling mists, brought into being by the little light I was carrying. I knew, too, that this little light was my consciousness, the only light I have. My own understanding is the sole treasure I possess, and the greatest' (*MDR* 93).

His dedication to scholarship, which was to remain with him all his life, became apparent in his student years, with the result that he qualified in the shortest possible time. Emerging from his social isolation, he joined the Basel branch of the Swiss student Zofingia Society, and began to discover his capacity to influence people through the force and originality of his ideas. Significantly, the title of the first paper he presented before the Society was 'On the Limits of the Exact Sciences' in which he attacked scientists for their inflexible materialism. In a later talk, he proposed that the soul, though immaterial and existing outside space and time, should nevertheless prove susceptible to empirical investigation through research into the phenomena of hypnotism, somnambulism, and mediumistic communication. His presentations drew large audiences and provoked lively discussion.

Determined to put his ideas to the test, he began while still a student to attend and record the seances of a young medium who was also a cousin, Hélène Preiswerk. His meticulously detailed observations collected over a period of two years subsequently formed the basis of his doctoral dissertation 'On the Psychology and Pathology of So-Called Occult Phenomena' presented at Basel University in 1902.

His approach to this subject was influenced by an earlier study by Theodore Flournoy (1854–1920) of a medium called Catherine Muller (better known under her pseudonym, Helen Smith), who, in the trance state, gave details of her previous lives. Flournoy concluded that her utterances were 'romances of the subliminal imagination', and that they were evidence of the myth-making powers of the unconscious mind.

Two aspects of his cousin's performances particularly impressed Jung. One was how real her 'spirits' seemed to her: 'I see them before me,' she told him, 'I can touch them, I speak to them about everything I wish as naturally as I'm talking to you. They must be real' (*CW* I, para. 43). The other was the way in which a quite different, more dignified personality emerged when Hélène was in a trance. Her 'control' spirit, who said her name was 'Ivenes', spoke in perfect High German instead of Hélène's customary Basel dialect. Jung concluded that 'Ivenes' was the mature, adult personality that was developing in Hélène's unconscious. The seances provided a means through which this development could proceed.

The importance of this study for Jung was greater than the doctorate it earned him. In it we can detect the origins of two ideas which were to become central to the practice of analytical psychology: (1) that part-personalities or 'complexes' existing in the unconscious psyche can 'personate' in trances, dreams, and hallucinations, and (2) that the real work of personality development proceeds at the unconscious level.

These ideas, in turn, gave rise to (1) a therapeutic technique (*active imagination*) and (2) a teleological concept (*individuation*): the notion that the goal of personal development is *wholeness*, i.e. to become as complete a human being as personal circumstances allow. We shall return to these issues later on.

Jung's decision to be a psychiatrist came towards the end of his medical studies when he dipped into Krafft-Ebing's *Textbook of Psychiatry*. The Preface alone had such an impact on him that his heart began to pound and he had to stand up to draw a deep breath. What excited him was Krafft-Ebing's description of the psychoses (major mental illnesses such as schizophrenia and severe manic-depression in which sufferers are deprived of their reason) as 'diseases of the personality' and his statement that books about psychiatry must, of necessity, be stamped with a subjective character.

Jung tells us that 'in a flash of illumination' he saw psychiatry as the only possible profession: 'Here alone the two currents of my interest could flow together and in a united stream dig their own bed. Here was the empirical field common to biological and spiritual facts, which I had everywhere sought and nowhere found. Here at last was the place where the collision of nature and spirit became a reality' (*MDR* 111).

Years of apprenticeship

When Jung informed his tutors and fellow students that he proposed to specialize in psychiatry, they were shocked, for they felt he would be wasting his talents: psychiatry was the least respected speciality in medicine and they believed Jung could have a promising future as a physician. 'My old wound, the feeling of being an outsider, and of alienating others, began to ache again' (*MDR* 111). However, having obtained his medical degree with distinction at the end of 1900, he had the good fortune to be taken on to the staff of the Burghölzli Psychiatric Hospital in Zürich as an assistant to Eugen Bleuler (1857–1939), one of the outstanding psychiatrists of his time, and destined to enter history as the originator of the term schizophrenia. The Burghölzli enjoyed an excellent reputation as the Psychiatric Clinic of Zürich University and Jung regarded the years he spent there as an invaluable apprenticeship. Bleuler was quick to recognize Jung's brilliance and did much to advance his career, promoting him to be his deputy, making him head of the out-patient department, and arranging his appointment as lecturer in psychiatry and psychotherapy at Zürich University. More important still, Bleuler set him to work on Galton's word-association test. This research was to earn Jung considerable fame in the world of psychology as well as the friendship of Sigmund Freud.

The word-association test, with which all students of psychology are familiar, was devised by Sir Francis Galton (1822–1911) and developed by Wilhelm Wundt (1832–1920). The procedure is simple. The experimenter reads out to the subject a series of words from a carefully prepared list, pausing after each word to allow the subject to respond with the first word that comes to mind. The response word is recorded together with the time, in seconds, taken to elicit the response. When all the words have been presented, the procedure is repeated, the subject being asked to respond with the same words as on the previous occasion.

One researcher who worked on the test before Jung, Theodor Ziehen, had already demonstrated that a prolonged reaction time occurred when a stimulus word was associated in the subject's mind with some disagreeable or disturbing idea. When all words resulting in delayed responses in a given subject were gathered together it was sometimes possible to detect in them a cluster of related ideas—what Ziehen called 'an emotionally charged complex of representations'. This finding particularly intrigued Jung because his work on Hélène Preiswerk's trances had already alerted him to the existence of part-personalities made up of dissociated unconscious components similar to those described as 'subconscious fixed ideas' by the French psychologist, Pierre Janet (1859–1947), under whom Jung studied briefly in Paris, on leave from the Burghölzli, in 1902. These Jung identified with Ziehen's 'complexes', and when he read Freud's *The Interpretation of Dreams* (1900) he recognized them again in the 'repressed wishes' and 'traumatic memories' which Freud held to be responsible for neurotic symptoms and for the content of dreams.

Jung says that dominating his research interests was one burning question: what actually takes place inside the mentally ill? Unlike the majority of psychiatrists before or since, he gave serious attention to what his schizophrenic patients actually said and did, and was able to demonstrate that their delusions, hallucinations, and gestures were not simply 'mad' but full of psychological meaning. For example, he discovered that one old lady, who had spent the fifty years of her incarceration in the Burghölzli making stitching movements as if she was sewing shoes, had been jilted by her lover just before she became ill: as Jung was able to discover, he was a cobbler.

Although Jung believed psychotic phenomena were associated with the presence of a biochemical toxin circulating in the patient's bloodstream, he nevertheless argued that schizophrenia could be understood in psychoanalytic terms as 'an introversion of libido'—the libido being withdrawn from the outer world of reality and invested in the inner world of myth-creation, fantasy, and dreams. The schizophrenic, he maintained, was a dreamer in a world awake. He published his observations in *The Psychology of Dementia Præcox* in 1907, which added to his already considerable reputation as a research psychiatrist.

Friendship with Freud

Realizing that his experimental findings provided objective support for Freud's theory of *repression*, Jung sent him a copy of his book *Studies in Word-Association* on its publication in 1906. Freud's enthusiastic response encouraged Jung to go to Vienna to meet him in March 1907. They got on so well that they talked without interruption for thirteen hours. There is no doubt that they were intellectually infatuated with one another and the friendship which blossomed between them, largely sustained by correspondence, lasted for nearly six years.

Like Bleuler, Freud was impressed by Jung's energy, enthusiasm, and commitment. He became powerfully attached to him, recognizing him as 'the ablest helper to have joined me thus far' and seeing him as his probable successor as leader of the psychoanalytic movement. Although Freud was only 50 when they met, he was something of a hypochondriac, and had a superstitious fear that he had only twelve years longer to live. Securing 'the succession' was thus a high priority for him, and, on the face of it, Jung was an excellent choice for the role. He had a first-rate mind, was a successful psychiatrist working at one of Europe's most respected hospitals, and, perhaps most important of all, he was not Viennese and he was not a Jew. Freud was acutely aware of the danger that anti-Semitism, associated with public disgust at his ideas on infantile sexuality, could result in the widespread rejection, or even suppression, of psychoanalysis, and he hoped that the adherence of a Swiss Christian of Jung's stature could help rescue his movement from this fate.

In addition, Jung was able to make significant contributions to psychoanalytic theory and practice. Not only did his word-association experiments provide hard empirical evidence for the existence and power of unconscious complexes, but his work with schizophrenics carried psychoanalytic concepts into areas beyond Freud's reach. (Freud trained as a neurologist and had little psychiatric experience, having worked only briefly as a *locum tenens* in a mental hospital.) Moreover, Jung infected Freud with his enthusiasm for the study of mythology and comparative religion, though with potentially disastrous consequences, for the conclusions that both men drew from these studies were explosively at variance with one another.

On Jung's side, the desire for Freud's friendship was as much personal as professional. In the older, more experienced man, he found a mentor—a distinguished colleague who represented the intellectually courageous father that his own father, the doubting theologian, was not. Both men understood this. 'Let me enjoy your friendship not as one between equals but as that of father and son,' wrote Jung soon after their first meeting. Freud responded at a later date by formally anointing Jung as his 'Son and Heir', his 'Crown Prince'. In fact, Freud needed a 'son' no less than Jung needed a 'father', but the kind of son Freud wanted was one who would be willing to defer unconditionally to his authority and to perpetuate, without modification, the doctrines and principles of his rule. For his part, Jung needed a father-figure through whose influence he could overcome his adolescent misgivings and discover his own masculine authority. Although Jung basked in Freud's approval and was flattered to be deemed a worthy successor to him, he knew

13

that he could not endorse Freud's ideas in their entirety. Nor could he sacrifice his intellectual integrity to a set of dogmas in the way that his father had done. He nevertheless acquiesced in Freud's wish that he should serve as the first president of the International Psychoanalytic Association when it was set up in 1910, and as chief editor of the first psychoanalytic journal, the *Jahrbuch*.

As time passed, Jung's differences with Freud became harder to conceal. Two of Freud's basic assumptions were unacceptable to him: (1) that human motivation is exclusively sexual and (2) that the unconscious mind is entirely personal and peculiar to the individual. Jung found these and other aspects of Freud's thinking reductionist and too narrow. Instead of conceiving psychic energy (or *libido* as Freud called it) as wholly sexual, Jung preferred to think of it as a more generalized 'life force', of which sexuality was but one mode of expression. Moreover, beneath the personal unconscious of repressed wishes and traumatic memories, posited by Freud, Jung believed there lay a deeper and more important layer that he was to call the *collective unconscious*, which contained *in potentia* the entire psychic heritage of mankind. The existence of this ancient basis of the mind had first been hinted to him as a child when he realized that there were things in his dreams that came from somewhere beyond himself. Its existence was confirmed when he studied the delusions and hallucinations of schizophrenic patients and found them to contain symbols and images which also occurred in myths and fairy-tales all over the world. He concluded that there must exist a dynamic psychic substratum, common to all humanity, on the basis of which each individual builds his or her private experience of life.

Whenever he attempted to express these ideas to Freud, however, they were attributed either to youthful inexperience or to *resistance*. 'Don't deviate too far from me when you are really so close to me, for if you do, we may one day be played off against one another,' Freud admonished him, adding: 'My inclination is to treat those colleagues who offer resistance exactly as we would treat patients in the same situation.' Jung was irked by such condescension, and it was inevitable, given the character of the two men, that a row would eventually break out between them. It was heralded in 1911 by the publication of the first part of Jung's

Transformations and Symbols of the Libido ('It is a risky business for an egg to be cleverer than the hen,' Jung wrote to Freud. 'Still what is in the egg must find the courage to creep out') and finally erupted in 1912 with publication of part two (in a letter to Freud Jung quoted Zarathustra: 'One repays a teacher badly if one remains only a pupil'). In this work, and in a series of lectures given in New York in September 1912, Jung spelt out the heretical view that libido was a much wider concept than Freud allowed and that it could appear in 'crystallized' form in the universal symbols or 'primordial images' apparent in the myths of humanity. Jung drew special attention to the myth of the hero, interpreting the recurrent theme of his fight with a dragon-monster as the struggle of the adolescent ego for deliverance from the mother. This led him to interpretations of the Oedipus complex and the incest taboo which were very different from those proposed by Freud. In Jung's view, a child became attached to his mother not because she was the object of incestuous passion, as Freud maintained, but because she was the provider of love and care—a view which anticipated the theoretical revolution wrought some forty years later by the British analyst and psychiatrist John Bowlby. Furthermore, Jung maintained that the incest taboo was primary: it existed a priori, and was not derived from the father's prohibition of the boy's lust for his mother, as Freud insisted. Oedipal longings, when they occurred, were the consequence of incest prohibition rather than its cause. Jung also argued that the Oedipus complex was not the universal phenomenon that Freud declared it to be.

In redefining libido as undifferentiated psychic energy Jung looked beyond psychology to parallels in physics, in particular to the theory of the transformation of energy as proposed by Robert Mayer. All psychological phenomena, like all physical phenomena, Jung argued, are *manifestations of energy* and this gives symbols their dynamic transformative power. We shall give further consideration to this propensity in Chapter 5.

Publication of these views provoked a major rift with Freud which resulted in the formal termination of their relationship early in 1913. Jung resigned his presidency of the Association, his editorship of the *Jahrbuch*, and his lectureship at the University of Zürich, and withdrew from the psychoanalytic movement. Once again, he was entirely on his own.

The manner in which their friendship ended was typical of them both. To Jung, the purpose of life was to realize one's own potential, to follow one's own perception of the truth, and to become a whole person in one's own right. This was the goal of *individuation*, as he later called it. If he was to keep faith with himself, he *had* to go his own way: it would have been impossible for him to spend his life playing second fiddle in a two-man band. As for Freud, belief in the correctness of his own theories was absolute, and this made him so intolerant of dissent that he usually ended up provoking it. He was a strange amalgam of autocrat and masochist: as he once admitted to Jung, his emotional life demanded the existence of an intimate friend and a hated enemy, and, not infrequently, he encountered both in the same person. This pattern was apparent in his childhood relationship with his nephew John (who happened to be his own age), and in the friendship which supported him through his period of 'splendid isolation' (1894–9, when he was conducting his self-analysis and establishing the principles of psychoanalysis) with Wilhelm Fliess. Freud's friendship with Jung, the quarrel, and Jung's subsequent loss to psychoanalysis constituted but one of a number of such painful episodes. A similar fate overtook Freud's relationship with Breuer, Adler, Stekel, Meynert, Silberer, Tausk, and Wilhelm Reich. Reich developed a psychosis, from which he recovered only temporarily, while Silberer and Tausk eventually committed suicide. For Jung the consequences were almost as dire, for he fell into a protracted 'state of disorientation', at times verging on psychosis, which lasted four or five years. Although profoundly disturbing, this proved to be a period of intense creativity which Jung referred to as his 'confrontation with the unconscious', and it was triggered as much by upheavals in his domestic life as by the loss of his friendship with Freud.

Married life

In 1903 Jung had married Emma Rauschenbach (1882–1955), the daughter of a rich industrialist. Between 1904 and 1914 they had five children: four daughters and a son. At first they lived in a flat in the Burghölzli. Then in 1908 they moved into a handsome house which they designed and built beside the lake at Küsnacht, and there they remained for the rest of their lives.

Emma Jung was an attractive, elegant woman, who, with her husband's encouragement, was destined to become a gifted analyst, lecturer, and author. She was an admirable wife and mother, and there can be no doubt that Jung loved her all his life. However, as he confessed to Freud, he recognized 'polygamous components' in himself, asserting that 'The pre-requisite of a good marriage, it seems to me, is the licence to be unfaithful' (*The Freud/Jung Letters*, 289; 30 January 1910).

Jung maintained that essentially two kinds of women are important for a man: on the one hand, he needs a wife to create his home, and to bear and rear his children; on the other, a *femme inspiratrice*, a spiritual companion, to share his fantasies and inspire his greatest works. This assertion probably resulted from a split in his own *anima* (the female complex in his unconscious) and the most likely explanation of this split derives from the period in his fourth year when, separated from his mother, he was looked after by a young maid from his father's parish. The latter made an indelible impression, and he still remembered her in his eighties:

She had black hair and an olive complexion, and was quite different from my mother. I can see her, even now, her hairline, her throat, with its darkly pigmented skin, and her ear. All this seemed to me very strange yet strangely familiar . . . This type of girl later became a component of my anima. The feeling of strangeness which she conveyed, and yet of having known her always, was a characteristic of that figure which later came to symbolize for me the whole essence of womanhood. (*MDR* 23)

This temporary nursemaid was the first embodiment of a maternal adjunct, the *femme inspiratrice*, the consolation of his lonely inner journeying. Although well content with Emma as a wife, his anima continued to demand the additional presence of a loving companion and confidante with whom to share his latest dreams and ideas. On at least two occasions this enticing figure was to present herself to him in the guise of a patient, briefly in the case of Sabina Spielrein (the first patient he treated successfully with Freud's methods) and, more lastingly, in Antonia Wolff, who became a lifelong intimate and colleague. In addition, Jung gathered round himself a number of female devotees (irreverently known to Zürich wits as the *Jungfrauen*), who came to Zürich to analyse and study with him and could seldom bring themselves to leave. It was as if the early separation from his mother had taught him that he could never trust the love of one woman and must always seek safety in numbers.

Understandably, Emma was not happy with this state of affairs, though with time, and out of necessity, she came to endure it. Jung's affair with Toni Wolff began sometime in 1910, and it caused a scandal when he insisted on bringing her, together with Emma, to the Weimar Conference of the International Psychoanalytic Association in 1911. There were bitter rows in which Jung resisted Emma's demands that he give up his extra-marital relationship, insisting that Toni was far too important for him to do without her. Since there could be no question of a divorce, Emma must adjust to the situation and accept Toni as an indispensable part of his life. Emma appears to have given way to him as much out of fear for his sanity as a determination to preserve her marriage. Certainly it was a traumatic time for both of them, and it may well have been a precipitating cause of the prolonged psychic disturbance which began to afflict Jung towards the end of 1913.

Confrontation with the unconscious

This started with a horrifying vision that recurred during the autumn of 1913 in which he saw the whole of Northern Europe flooded by a sea of blood. This was followed by dreams in which all Europe had been frozen by an Arctic wave and in which he shot and killed the Teutonic hero Siegfried as he rode past in a chariot. 'An incessant stream of fantasies had been released . . . I was living in a constant state of tension; often I felt as if gigantic blocks of stone were tumbling down upon me. One thunderstorm followed another' (*MDR* 170–1).

At times the disturbance was so severe as to bring him to the edge of madness. He played in his garden like a child, heard voices in his head, walked about holding conversations with imaginary figures, and, during one episode, believed his house to be crowded with the spirits of the dead. Yet it is a measure of his unusual qualities that he regarded this disaster *as if is were an experiment being performed on him*: a psychiatrist was having a breakdown thus providing a golden opportunity for research. He could study the whole experience at first hand and then use it to help his patients.

This idea—that I was committing myself to a dangerous enterprise not for myself alone, but also for the sake of my patients—helped me over several critical phases . . . It is, of course, ironical that I, a psychiatrist, should at almost every step in my experiment have run into the same psychic material which is the stuff of psychosis and is found in the insane. This is the fund of unconscious images which fatally confuse the mental patient. But it is also the matrix of a mythopoeic imagination which has vanished from our rational age.   (*MDR* 172, 181)

The dream of killing Siegfried suggested to him that the conscious ideals embodied in this heroic figure with whom his No. 1 personality had identified itself, were no longer appropriate and had to be sacrificed, 'for there are higher things than the ego's will, and to these one must bow' (*MDR* 174). He turned inwards to encounter his No. 2 personality and gave free rein to the powerful energies he found there.

In order to seize hold of the fantasies, I frequently imagined a steep descent. I even made several attempts to get to the very bottom. The first time I reached, as it were, a depth of about a thousand feet; the next time I found myself at the edge of a cosmic abyss. It was like a voyage to the moon, or a descent into empty space. First came the image of a crater, and I had the feeling that I was in the land of the dead. The atmosphere was that of the other world.   (*MDR* 174)

This method of seizing hold of the fantasies was much later used by him as a therapeutic technique in his analytic practice. He called it *active imagination*, and its discovery owed much to the example of his mediumistic cousin, Hélène Preiswerk. Going down the steep descent was akin to entering a state of trance during which unconscious personalities emerged with sufficient clarity for him to hold conversations with them. Essentially, what he had discovered was a knack—the knack of descending into the underworld, like Odysseus, Heracles, or Orpheus, while remaining fully conscious. Two of the figures he regularly encountered on these excursions were a beautiful young woman called Salome and an old man with a white beard and the wings of a kingfisher called Philemon. Jung came to see these as the embodiment of two archetypes—the eternal feminine and the wise old man.

His conversations with these figures brought him the crucial insight that things happen in the psyche that are not produced by conscious intention: they possess a life of their own.

Philemon represented a force which was not myself. In my fantasies I held conversations with him, and he said things which I had not consciously thought. For I observed clearly that it was he who spoke, not I. He said I treated thoughts as if I generated them myself, but in his view thoughts were like animals in the forest, or people in a room, or birds in the air, and added, 'If you should see people in a room, you would not think that you had made those people, or that you were responsible for them.' It was he who taught me psychic objectivity, the reality of the psyche. (*MDR* 176)

By 'the reality of the psyche' Jung meant that he understood the psyche to be an a priori fact of nature, an objective phenomenon which is irreducible to any factor other than itself. 'Psychic existence is the only category of existence of which we have *immediate* knowledge, since nothing can be known unless it first appears as a psychic image' (*CW* XI, para. 769). Like 'Ivenes' for Hélène, Philemon inhered Jung's own potential for maturity. 'At times he seemed to me quite real, as if he were a living personality. I went up and down the garden with him, and to me he was what the Indians call a guru' (*MDR* 176). Far from being destructive psychotic phenomena, these conversations with Philemon helped Jung to discover a new security. Having lost his outer father-figures in the form of Bleuler and Freud and destroyed their heroic representative in the shape of Siegfried, he now found his own inner authority in Philemon. Moreover, Philemon was the first clear manifestation of the richly charismatic personality Jung was destined to become—the wise old man of Küsnacht.

That such experiences did not tip him over into a full-blown psychosis may well have been due to the attitude he adopted to them: he says that he took great care to record every detail of what occurred to him, first in what came to be known as the Black Book, consisting of six black-bound notebooks, the contents of which he later transferred to the Red Book, a folio volume bound in red leather, written in Gothic script, and embellished with illustrations.

One day while engaged in this work he heard a female voice say that what he was doing was not science but 'art'. He was intensely irritated by this and expostulated, 'No, it is not art! On the contrary, it is nature.' He resented the suggestion that he was engaged in an artistic activity because this would imply that his experiences were wilfully contrived and not the spontaneous eruptions from the unconscious that he took them to be. However, he reflected deeply on the existence of this inner woman who possessed the power to upset him, and concluded that she must be the personification of his soul. 'Later I came to see that this inner feminine figure plays a typical, or archetypal, role in the unconscious of a man, and I called her the "anima" ' (*MDR* 179).

The whole crisis resolved itself during the months immediately following the Armistice in 1918 when Jung served as the commandant of a camp for British internees. The duties were not onerous and he spent his mornings working on a series of spontaneous drawings which seemed to express his psychic state at the time. He subsequently realized that these drawings resembled ancient mandalas. Mandalas have been found all over the world and are primordial images of wholeness or totality. Although circular, they commonly incorporate some representation of quaternity, such as a cross or a square. The centre usually contains a reference to a deity. Jung began to understand these as representations of the *Self*, the central nucleus of the personality, which he sometimes referred to as the 'archetype of archetypes'. He found that his mandala drawings enabled him to give objective form to the psychic transformations that he underwent from day to day. 'I had a distinct feeling that they were something central, and in time I acquired through them a living conception of the Self' (*MDR* 187).

Finally, there was a dream which had an extraordinary impact on him. He found himself in Liverpool (lit. 'pool of life'), a city whose quarters were arranged radially about a square. In the centre was a round pool with a small island in the middle. The island blazed with sunlight while everything round it was obscured by rain, fog, smoke, and dimly-lit darkness. On the island stood a single tree, a magnolia, in a shower of reddish blossoms. Although the tree stood in the sunlight, Jung felt that it was, at the same time, itself the source of light.

This seemed to sum up all he had been through, and to symbolize the point he had reached. 'When I parted from Freud, I knew that I was plunging into the unknown. Beyond Freud, after all, I knew nothing; but I had taken the step into darkness. When that happens, and then such a dream comes, one feels it as an act of grace' (*MDR* 190).

When they were over, he regarded the years of his 'experiment' as the most important of his life: 'in them everything essential was decided' (*MDR* 191). They determined the future course of his development and were to provide him with the basis of the psychotherapeutic discipline that bears his name. 'It all began then; the later details are only supplements and clarifications of the material that burst forth from the unconscious, and at first swamped me. It was the *prima materia* for a lifetime's work' (*MDR* 191).

Creative illness

There has been much discussion about what actually happened to Jung during this critical phase of his life. One of the most persuasive interpretations is that of Henri Ellenberger, who, in his encyclopaedic *The Discovery of the Unconscious* (1970), suggests that Jung underwent a form of 'creative illness' similar to that suffered by Freud at an identical period (i.e. between the ages of 38 and 43).

The illness is prone to strike after a time of intense intellectual activity and resembles a neurosis or, in severe cases, a psychosis. Still struggling with the issues that were a prelude to the condition, the sufferer grows convinced that he is beyond outside help, becomes socially isolated, and turns deeper into himself. The disturbance can last four or five years. When recovery sets in it occurs spontaneously, and is associated with euphoria and a transformation of the personality. The subject feels that he has gained insight into important truths and believes that he has a duty to share these with the world. Thus, Jung observed:

there were things in the images which concerned not only myself but many others also. It was then that I ceased to belong to myself alone, ceased to have a right to do so. From then on my life belonged to the generality . . . It was then that I dedicated myself to the service of the psyche. I loved it and hated it, but it was my greatest wealth.   *(MDR* 184)

Jung's experience was similar to that undergone by shamans and religious mystics, as well as some artists, writers, and philosophers. Examples include van Gogh, Strindberg, Nietzsche, Theodor Fechner (the founder of psychophysics), and the theosophist, Rudolph Steiner. Jung himself compared it to Odysseus' *Nekyia* (his visit to the Sojourn of the Dead) and it was prefigured in the fantasies of Miss Miller (which formed the basis of his book *Transformations and Symbols of the Libido*) as much as by the trance performances of Hélène Preiswerk and Helen Smith. In Miss Miller's case, Jung has detected first a 'renunciation of the world' (associated with an introversion and regression of libido) followed by an 'acceptance of the world' (associated with an extraversion of libido and a more mature adaptation to outer reality). The theme of the descent into the underworld and the return also occurs in the epic of Gilgamesh, Virgil's *Aeneid*, and Dante's *Divine Comedy*. But the most interesting parallel is, as we have already noted, the neurotic breakdown suffered by Freud in the 1890s which he cured with his own self-analysis, discovering in the process the basic principles of psychoanalysis—the use of free association and dream analysis, the role of sexuality in the aetiology of neurotic illnesses, the stages of libidinal development in childhood, the fixation and regression of libido, the repression of forbidden wishes, and so on.

On their recovery, both men published major and original books: Freud's *The Interpretation of Dreams* appeared in 1900 when he was 45, and Jung's *Psychological Types* in 1921 when he was 46. Thus it was that most of Freud's ideas were already developed and had become fixed before he met Jung, whilst most of Jung's were developed after he had found the courage to part company from Freud and suffer the consequences of his loss. If the six years of their friendship was a period of discovery and preparation for Jung, for Freud it was a time of retrenchment, during which he became increasingly intolerant of those who would revise his ideas, which for him had become matters of indisputable fact.

Gregory Bateson (*Steps to an Ecology of Mind*, 1973) was not wrong when he described Jung's *Nekyia* as an *epistemological* crisis, during which he threw off Freud's reductionist theories and established the groundwork for his own. With the energy of one emerging from a creative illness, he returned to the study of myth, philosophy, and religion to find objective parallels to what he had experienced. *Psychological Types* was the fruit of this labour. In this book he began to organize his ideas about the structure and function of the psyche and to examine the basis of his differences (and Adler's differences) with Freud. He argued that in the course of development people come to adopt habitual attitudes which determine their experience of life. From a wide-ranging review of cultural history he concluded that two fundamental psychological orientations are apparent, which he called *introverted* and *extraverted attitudes*. Introversion is characterized by an inward movement of interest away from the outer world to the inner world of the subject, extraversion by an outward movement of interest away from the subject to the outer realm of objective reality. Jung believed that his differences with Freud were due to his own introversion working in opposition to Freud's extraversion.

This explanation contains more than a grain of truth, but it did not give sufficient weight to other no less important factors. Both men were products of very different backgrounds. Freud, an urban Jew, doted on as a child by a young and beautiful mother, was educated in a progressive tradition that led him naturally into science; while Jung, a rural Protestant, insecurely bonded to a depressed, sometimes absent, mother, was steeped in theology and Romantic idealism. Consequently, it is not surprising that Freud should be a sceptical empiricist and that he should believe in the universal significance of the Oedipus complex, while Jung retained a commitment to the life of the spirit and held that the Oedipus complex had no universal validity.

Another important distinction between them was Freud's habitual tendency to look backwards, which gave him a reductive concern with origins, and Jung's tendency to look forwards, which gave him an adaptive concern with goals. This distinction is apparent in their respective approaches to art as well as to mental illness. Jung came to the nub of the matter when rehearsing his differences with Freud in an article he wrote in 1920: 'Philosophical criticism has helped me to see that every psychology—my own included—has the character of a subjective confession,' he wrote. 'Even when I am dealing with empirical data, I am necessarily speaking about myself' (*CW* IV, para. 774). The same was true of Freud.

Individuation: the realization of the Self

For the rest of his life Jung was preoccupied with the dynamics of personal transformation and growth. He was one of the few psychologists in the twentieth century to maintain that development extends beyond childhood and adolescence through mid-life and into old age. It was this lifelong developmental process that he called *individuation*, and he believed that it could be brought to its highest fruition if one worked with and *confronted* and unconscious in the manner he had discovered in the course of his *Nekyia*.

What did he mean by confronting the unconscious? He experienced the unconscious as a living, numinous presence, the constant companion of every waking (and sleeping) moment. For him, the secret of life's meaning lay in relating to this daemonic power in such a way as to *know* it. To this secret the first sentence of his autobiography alerts us like a fanfare of trumpets: 'My life is the story of the self-realization of the unconscious.' How can we enable the unconscious to realize itself? By granting it freedom of expression and then examining what it has expressed. Thus, self-realization requires the psyche to turn round on itself and *confront* what it produces. In conducting this experiment Jung again experienced himself as split in two—between the conscious *subject*, who experienced, recorded, and struggled to survive, and the unconscious *other*, manifesting in the personalities and powers that forced themselves on him, demanding his attention and respect. Two consequences followed: a heightening of consciousness, and recognition of the psyche as a real, objective entity.

As it turned out he was a good advertisement for his own theories. Many have testified to the change that came over him as he entered middle age. The rather aloof, prickly young man gradually gave place to the wise, genial figure of his late maturity. Though never losing his taste for seclusion, he developed a talent for getting on with people in all walks of life, and those who came to consult or visit him were impressed as much by his courtesy and humour as by his wisdom and the quality of his mind. It was the

25

degree of individuation achieved by him that drew people to Zürich from all over the world, that attracted millions when they saw him on television in old age, and which accounts for the interest that has grown in him since he died.

He never ceased to work with the unconscious or to pursue his research into the material he had collected during his 'confrontation'. In 1922 he purchased some land at Bollingen, beside the beautiful upper lake of Zürich, and here he built a simple tower, round which he was to construct additions at various times during the rest of his life, turning it into an architectural mandala. At the heart of this intimate complex of stone, he reserved a room which only he was allowed to enter and there he accomplished his most important work both on himself and on his Psychology. At the end of his life he wrote: 'At Bollingen I am in the midst of my true life, I am most deeply myself' (*MDR* 214). It was the fulfilment in actuality of his childhood fantasy of the castle keep with its secret laboratory.

One crucial event that occurred after his mid-life crisis was his 'discovery' of alchemy. This happened in 1927 when the sinologist Richard Wilhelm sent him a German translation of a Taoist alchemical treatise called *The Secret of the Golden Flower*, requesting that he should write a commentary on it. As he read it, Jung realized with mounting excitement that he had found a historical parallel to his own experience: here was the most extraordinary and unexpected confirmation of his insights into the meaning of the mandala, the circumambulation of the centre, and the phenomenology of the Self. 'That was the first event which broke through my isolation,' he wrote (*MDR* 189). He was struck by the extraordinary affinity he felt with this rich psychic material, coming as it did from a source so remote from himself, and it set in train the series of alchemical investigations which were to absorb much of the life that was left to him.

Two dreams prepared him for what was in store. In one he discovered a seventeenth-century library in a previously unknown annexe to his house; and in the other some gates clanged shut behind him, trapping him in the same century. Patiently he began to assemble one of the largest collections of alchemical texts in existence, and it became clear to him that the alchemists had used a secret language which they expressed in arcane symbols. At first he understood little of what they signified, but as he worked along philological lines, compiling an elaborate lexicon of key phrases and cross-references, 'the alchemical mode of expression gradually yielded up its meaning' (*MDR* 196).

In alchemy, Jung realized, he had found a precursor of his own Psychology. 'The experiences of the alchemists were, in a sense, my experiences, and their world my world. This was, of course, a momentous discovery: I had stumbled upon the historical counterpart of my psychology of the unconscious' (*MDR* 196). Hitherto, alchemy had been dismissed as no more than a crude anticipation of chemistry, but Jung believed that, in their efforts to turn base metals into gold, the alchemists were symbolically engaged in a process of psychic transformation. In other words, alchemy was a metaphor for individuation.

Just as nature abhors a vacuum, so, in matters where one knows nothing, imagination will rush in to fill the void. Confronted by a field of ignorance, we project into it our own psychic activity and fill it up with meaning. Psychological *projection tests* make use of this propensity by inviting subjects to report what they see in ink blots or ambiguous figures. Leonardo da Vinci advocated a similar technique for inspiring landscapes by staring at wet patches on a wall. Jung was the first to recognize such practices as a useful means for studying otherwise inaccessible contents of the psyche: they enable us to become aware of new meanings arising from the unconscious by seeing them mirrored in outer reality; and this provides the key to one of the most valuable functions of art therapy. The alchemists, Jung realized, were, without knowing it, making use of the same mechanism: alchemy was an elaborate discipline based entirely upon the psychological phenomenon of *projection*.

Accounts of the stages through which the transformations of the alchemical opus progressed particularly fascinated Jung for he saw in them direct parallels to the stages of analysis. In the relationship between the alchemist and his female assistant, the *soror mystica*, Jung also detected an early model of the transference and countertransference relationship which develops between the analyst and patient in the course of analytic treatment. The discovery that alchemical symbols occur spontaneously in dreams, even in those of a modern scientist, confirmed for him the validity of his insight that archetypal psychic factors determined alchemical symbolism, and he published a series of such dreams (provided by the physicist and Nobel Laureate, Wolfgang Pauli, 1900–58) in *Psychology and Alchemy* (*CW* XII).

These researches renewed his commitment to analysis, which he now conceived more as a means to produce personal growth than as a technique for treating mental disorder, and he increasingly devoted his energy to teaching others, whether as pupils or patients, the same methods he had perfected during his own confrontation with the unconscious and which he had excavated in all their bizarre ambiguity from an occult science of the seventeenth century.

Ageing and growth

What distinguishes the Jungian approach to developmental psychology from virtually all others is the idea that even in old age we are growing towards realization of our full potential. This certainly appears to have been true of Jung himself. If, like so many of his European contemporaries, he had died during the First World War, we should have heard very little of him. As it was, his reputation flourished as he *grew* into old age. Not only were his most influential books published in the latter part of his life but his intellectual horizons continued to widen, as can be judged from the variety of subjects to which he turned his attention— synchronicity and flying saucers, for example, as well as psychotherapy, alchemy, the *I Ching*, and religion. For Jung, ageing was not a process of inexorable decline but a time for the progressive refinement of what is essential. 'The decisive question for a man is: is he related to something infinite or not?' (*MDR* 300). This insight was at the root of his life and his Psychology. The infinite, the eternal, the imperishable were ever present and imminent for him as the bedrock of reality, all the more fascinating for being hidden ('occult'). 'Life has always seemed to me like a plant that lives on its rhizome. The part that appears above ground lasts only a single summer. Then it withers away— an ephemeral apparition . . . Yet I have never lost a sense of something that lives and endures underneath the eternal flux. What we see is the blossom that passes. The rhizome remains'

(*MDR* 18). The great secret is to embody something essential in our lives. Then, undefeated by age, we can proceed with dignity and meaning, and, as the end approaches, be ready 'to die with life'. For the goal of old age is not senility, but wisdom.

The productive vitality of Jung's late maturity was heralded by a second 'creative illness'. Early in 1944, when he was 68, he suffered emboli in his heart and lungs which nearly killed him. As he lay in hospital he had a near-death experience in which he saw the earth from a thousand miles out in space. He felt he was detaching himself from the world and was resentful when his physician brought him back to life. Nevertheless, he made a full recovery, and threw himself into his writing which, for the next seventeen years, took precedence over all other activities. The illness seems to have carried a stage further the transition from his No. 1 to his No. 2 personality. This was confirmed for him by two dreams. In the first he saw a yogi, in lotus posture, deep in meditation. Jung realized that the yogi possessed his own face, and awoke in alarm. 'Aha, so he is the one who is meditating me,' he thought. 'He has a dream, and I am it.' In a second dream, which came much later, he experienced himself as the *projection* of an unknown flying object shaped like an old-fashioned magic lantern. He understood these dreams as showing that the unconscious is the generator of the empirical personality and that the Self assumes human shape in order to enter three-dimensional reality.

At the age of 82 he wrote:

In the end, the only events of my life worth telling are those when the imperishable world erupted into this transitory one . . . All other memories of travels, people and my surroundings have paled beside these interior happenings . . . But my encounters with the 'other' reality, my bouts with the unconscious, are indelibly engraved on my memory. In that realm there has always been wealth in abundance, and everything else has lost importance by comparison. (*MDR* 18)

The major themes that preoccupied Jung up to the end of his life were the mystery of opposites, their division, their union, and their transcendence, and the cosmic significance of human consciousness. He recorded his reflections in three difficult and challenging books: *Aion* (1951), *Answer to Job* (1952), and *Mysterium Coniunctionis* (1955–6). *Answer to Job*, the most accessible of these, brought him into conflict with theologians, for in it he denounced God for burdening humanity with responsibility for all the evil in the world while absolving Himself of all blame. This lack of self-awareness on the part of the Almighty, Jung argued, can only be corrected by human consciousness, and it explains why God found it necessary to incarnate Himself in man. 'That is the meaning of divine service, or the service that man can render to God, that light may emerge from the darkness, that the Creator may become conscious of His creation, and man conscious of himself' (*MDR* 312).

The germ of this insight came to him in 1925 on a visit to the Athai Plains in East Africa. With his travelling companions he stood on a hill looking down on the savannah stretching to the far horizon, gigantic herds of gazelle, antelope, gnu, zebra, and warthog grazing and moving forwards like slow rivers.

There was scarcely any sound save the melancholy cry of a bird of prey. This was the stillness of the eternal beginning, the world as it had always been, in the state of non-being; for until then no one had been present to know that it was this world. I walked away from my companions until I had put them out of sight, and savoured the feeling of being entirely alone. There I was now, the first human being to recognize that this was the world, but who did not know that in this moment he had first really created it.

There the cosmic meaning of consciousness became overwhelmingly clear to me. 'What nature leaves imperfect, the art perfects,' say the alchemists. Man, I, in an invisible act of creation put the stamp of perfection on the world by giving it objective existence . . . Now I knew what it was, and knew even more: that man is indispensable for the completion of creation; that, in fact, he himself is the second creator of the world, who alone has given to the world its objective existence—without which, unheard, unseen, silently eating, giving birth, dying, heads nodding through hundreds of millions of years, it would have gone on in the profoundest night of non-being down to its unknown end. Human consciousness created objective existence and meaning, and man found his indispensable place in the great process of being. (*MDR* 240–1)

Thus Jung's psychology became also a cosmology, for he saw the journey of personal development towards fuller consciousness as occurring in the context of eternity. The psyche, existing *sui generis* as an objective part of nature, is subject to the same laws that govern the universe and is itself the supreme fulfilment of those laws: through the miracle of consciousness, the human psyche provides the mirror in which Nature sees herself reflected.

In old age he had many premonitions of approaching death and what impressed him was the lack of fuss the unconscious makes about it. Indeed, death seemed to him to be a goal in itself, something to be welcomed. Thus, in one dream he saw 'the other Bollingen' bathed in a glow of light, and a voice told him that it was complete and ready to receive him. Looking back on his life he reflected, 'In my case it must have been a passionate urge to under-standing that brought about my birth. For that is the strongest element in my nature' (*MDR* 297). This need to understand and to *know* kept him creatively alive well into his eighty-sixth year, when he suffered two strokes within a week of one another and died peacefully on 6 June 1961 at Küsnacht.

2 Archetypes and the collective unconscious

In 1909 Jung and Freud were both invited to lecture at Clark University in Worcester, Massachusetts. They were away for seven weeks and they spent long periods every day talking and working on each other's dreams. Of all the dreams they analysed, two were to be critical for their friendship. The first was one of Freud's, which Jung did his best to interpret on the basis of only a few associations from Freud. When Jung pressed him for more, Freud looked rather suspiciously at him and declined: 'I cannot risk my authority,' he said. At that moment, commented Jung, he lost it altogether. 'That sentence burned itself into my memory; and in it the end of our relationship was already foreshadowed. Freud was placing personal authority above truth' (*MDR* 154).

The other dream was one of Jung's. He dreamt that he was on the top floor of an old house, well furnished and with fine paintings on the walls. He marvelled that this should be his house and thought 'Not bad!' But then it occurred to him that he had no idea what the lower floor was like, so he went down to see. There everything was much older. The furnishings were medieval and everything was rather dark. He thought, 'Now I really must explore the whole house.' He looked closely at the floor. It was made of stone slabs, and in one of these he discovered a ring. When he pulled it, the slab lifted, and he saw some narrow stone steps leading down into the depths. He went down and entered a low cave cut out of the rock. Bones and broken pottery were scattered about in the dust, the remains of a primitive culture, and he found two human skulls, obviously very old and half-disintegrated. Then he awoke.

All that interested Freud about this dream was the possible identity of the skulls. He wanted Jung to say who they belonged to, for it seemed evident to him that Jung must harbour a death-wish against their owners. Jung felt this was completely beside the point, but, as was habitual with him at that stage in the relationship, he kept his doubts to himself. To Jung, the house was an image of the psyche. The room on the upper floor represented his conscious personality. The ground floor stood for the first level of the unconscious, which he was to call the *personal* unconscious, while in the deepest level of all he reached the *collective* unconscious. There he discovered the world of the *primitive man within himself*. To him, the skulls had nothing to do with death-wishes. They belonged to our human ancestors, who helped shape the common psychic heritage of us all.

When he finally summoned up the courage to announce his hypothesis of a collective unconscious, it proved to be his most significant departure from Freud, and his most important single contribution to psychology. Although Freud did make some passing reference to there being 'archaic vestiges' in the psyche, he remained intractably resistant to the enormous implications of Jung's bold and revolutionary idea.

What Jung was proposing was no less than a fundamental concept on which the whole science of psychology could be built. Potentially, it is of comparable importance to quantum theory in physics. Just as the physicist investigates particles and waves, and the biologist genes, so Jung held it to be the business of the psychologist to investigate the collective unconscious and the functional units of which it is composed—the *archetypes*, as he eventually called them. Archetypes are 'identical psychic structures common to all' (*CW* V, para. 224), which together constitute 'the archaic heritage of humanity' (*CW* V, para. 259). Essentially, he conceived them to be innate neuropsychic centres possessing the capacity to initiate, control, and mediate the common behavioural characteristics and typical experiences of all human beings. Thus, on appropriate occasions, archetypes give rise to similar thoughts, images, mythologems, feelings, and ideas in people, irrespective of their class, creed, race, geographical location, or historical epoch. An individual's entire archetypal endowment makes up the collective unconscious, whose authority and power is vested in a central nucleus, responsible for integrating the whole personality, which Jung termed the Self.

Jung never disagreed with Freud's view that personal experience is of crucial significance for the development of each individual, but he denied that this development occurred in an unstructured personality. On the contrary, for Jung, the role of personal experi-

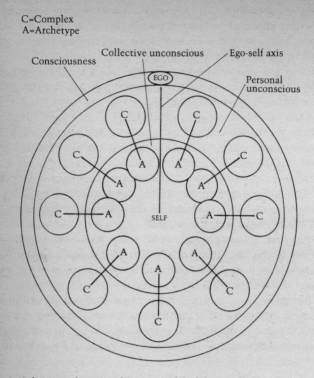

FIG. 1. Schematic diagram of Jung's model of the psyche

ence was *to develop what is already there*—to activate the archetypal potential already present in the Self. Our psyches are not
simply a product of experience, any more than our bodies are
merely the product of what we eat.

A diagrammatic representation of Jung's model of the psyche
(Fig. 1) will help to make this clear. The model should be visualized
as a globe or a sphere, like a three-layered onion. At the centre, and ·
permeating the entire system with its influence, is the Self. Within
the inner of the three concentric circles, is the collective unconscious, composed of archetypes. The outer circle represents consciousness, with its focal ego orbiting the system rather like a
planet orbiting the sun, or the moon orbiting the earth. Interme-
diate between the conscious and the collective unconscious, is the

personal unconscious, made up of complexes, each of which is linked to an archetype: for complexes are *personifications* of archetypes; they are the means through which archetypes manifest themselves in the personal psyche.

To a limited extent Jung's archetypes resemble Plato's *ideas*. For Plato, 'ideas' were pure mental forms existing in the minds of the gods before human life began and were consequently above and beyond the ordinary world of phenomena. They were *collective* in the sense that they embodied the *general* characteristics of a thing, but they were also implicit in its *specific* manifestations. The human fingerprint, for example, is instantly recognizable for what it is on account of its unmistakable configuration of contours and whorls. Yet every fingerprint has a configuration unique to its owner, which is why those who turn their hands to burglary must remember to wear gloves if they wish to escape detection and arrest. Archetypes similarly combine the universal with the individual, the general with the unique, in that they are common to all humanity, yet nevertheless manifest themselves in every human being in a way peculiar to him or to her.

Where Jung's archetypes differ from Plato's ideas is in their dynamic, goal-seeking properties. Archetypes actively seek their actualization in the personality and the behaviour of the individual, as the life cycle unfolds in the context of the environment.

The actualization of archetypes

The most important archetype to be actualized in the personal psyche of a child is the mother archetype. Actualization (Jung also speaks of 'evocation', and 'constellation') of an archetype seems to proceed in accordance with the laws of association worked out by psychologists at the end of the nineteenth century. Two of these laws are particularly apposite: they are the law of *similarity* and the law of *contiguity*. Thus, the mother archetype is actualized in the child's psyche through the *contiguity* of a female caretaker whose behaviour and personal characteristics are sufficiently *similar* to the built-in structure of the maternal archetype for the child to perceive her and experience her as 'mother'. Then, as the attachment relationship develops, the archetype becomes active in the personal psyche of the child in the form of the mother *complex*. At the same time, through similarity and contiguity, the infant constellates the child archetype in the mother. Each partner of this dyad creates the perceptual field responsible for evoking the archetype in the other.

Throughout Jung's lifetime, most psychologists maintained that children were passive recipients of maternal care and that they became attached to their mothers because they were fed by them (the so-called 'cupboard love' theory). Jung maintained, on the contrary, that children actively participated in the formation of all their relationships with the world, insisting that it was 'a mistake to suppose [as did the majority of his contemporaries] that the psyche of the newborn child is a *tabula rasa* in the sense that there is absolutely nothing in it' (*CW* IX. i, para. 136). We bring with us an innate psychic structure enabling us to have the experiences typical of our kind.

Thus the whole nature of man presupposes woman, both physically and spiritually. His system is tuned into woman from the start, just as it is prepared for a quite definite world where there is water, light, air, salt, carbohydrate, etc. The form of the world into which he is born is already inborn in him as a virtual image. Likewise parents, wife, children, birth, and death are inborn in him as virtual images, as psychic aptitudes. These *a priori* categories have by nature a collective character; they are images of parents, wife, and children *in general*, and are not individual predestinations. We must therefore think of these images as lacking in solid content, hence as unconscious. They only acquire solidity, influence, and eventual consciousness in the encounter with empirical facts, which touch the unconscious aptitude and quicken it to life. They are, in a sense, the deposits of all our ancestral experiences, but they are not the experiences themselves. (*CW* VII, para. 300)

All those factors, therefore, that were essential to our near and remote ancestors will also be essential to us, for they are embedded in the inherited organic system. (*CW* VIII, para. 717)

Very similar ideas to Jung's have become current in the last forty years in the relatively new science of ethology (that branch of behavioural biology which studies animals in their natural habitats). Every animal species possesses a repertoire of behaviours. This behavioural repertoire is dependent on structures which evolution has built into the central nervous system of the species. Ethologists call these structures *innate releasing mechanisms*, or IRMs. Each IRM is primed to become active when an appropriate stimulus—called a *sign stimulus*—is encountered in the environment. When such a stimulus appears, the innate mechanism is released, and the animal responds with a characteristic *pattern of behaviour* which is adapted, through evolution, to the situation. Thus, a mallard duck becomes amorous at the sight of the handsome green head of a mallard drake, the green head being the *sign stimulus* which releases in the duck's central nervous system the *innate mechanism* responsible for the characteristic *patterns of behaviour* associated with courtship in the duck.

This is very much how Jung conceived of archetypes operating in human beings, and he was aware of the comparison. An archetype, he said, is not 'an inherited idea' but rather 'an inherited mode of functioning, corresponding to the inborn way in which the chick emerges from the egg, the bird builds its nest, a certain kind of wasp stings the motor ganglion of the caterpillar, and eels find their way to the Bermudas. In other words, it is a "pattern of behaviour". This aspect of the archetype,' concludes Jung, 'the purely biological one, is the proper concern of scientific psychology' (*CW* XVIII, para. 1228). In a sense, ethology and Jungian psychology can be viewed as two sides of the same coin: it is as if ethologists have been engaged in an extraverted exploration of the archetype and Jungians in an introverted examination of the IRM.

The currency of archetypal theory

Many other disciplines have produced concepts similar to the archetypal hypothesis, but usually without reference to Jung. For example, the primary concern of Claude Lévi-Strauss and the French school of structural anthropology is with the unconscious *infrastructures* which they hold responsible for all human customs and institutions; specialists in linguistics maintain that although grammars differ from one another, their basic forms—which Noam Chomsky calls their *deep structures*—are universal (i.e. at the deepest neuropsychic level, there exists a universal [or 'archetypal'] grammar on which all individual grammars are based); an entirely new discipline, sociobiology, has grown up on the theory that the patterns of behaviour typical of all social species, the human species included, are dependent on *genetically transmitted response strategies* designed to maximize the fitness of the organism to survive in the environment in which it evolved; sociobiology also holds that the psycho-social development in individual members of a species is dependent on what are termed *epigenetic rules* (*epi* = upon, *genesis* = development; i.e. rules upon which development proceeds); more recently still, ethologically oriented psychiatrists have begun to study what they call *psychobiological response patterns* and *deeply homologous neural structures* which they hold responsible for the achievement of healthy or unhealthy patterns of adjustment in individual patients in response to variations in their social environment. All these concepts are compatible with the archetypal hypothesis which Jung had proposed decades earlier to virtually universal indifference.

This raises an important question. If Jung's theory of archetypes is so fundamental that it keeps being rediscovered by the practitioners of many other disciplines, why did it not receive the enthusiastic welcome it deserved when Jung proposed it? The explanation is, I think, twofold: namely, the time at which Jung stated the theory, and the way in which he published it.

In the first place, throughout Jung's mature lifetime, researchers working in university departments of psychology were in the grip of behaviourism, which discounted innate or genetic factors, preferring to view the individual as a *tabula rasa* whose development was almost entirely dependent on environmental factors. Jung's contrary view that the infant comes into the world with an intact blueprint for life which it then proceeds to implement through interaction with the environment, was so at variance with the prevailing *Zeitgeist* as to guarantee it a hostile reception.

Secondly, Jung did not state his theory in a clear, testable form, nor did he back it up with sufficiently persuasive evidence. His book *Transformations and Symbols of the Libido* in which he first put forward his idea of a collective unconscious giving rise to 'primordial images' (as he originally called archetypes) was so densely written and so packed with mythological exegesis as to make it virtually impenetrable to any but the most determined reader. Moreover, in arguing that 'primordial images' were derived from the past history of mankind, Jung exposed himself to the accusation that he, like Freud, subscribed to the discredited theory of the *inheritance of acquired characteristics*, originally proposed by Jean-Baptiste Lamarck (1744–1829), i.e. that ideas or images

occurring in members of one generation could be passed on genetically to the next and subsequent generations.

In fact, the collective unconscious is a respectable scientific
hypothesis and one does not have to adopt a Lamarckian view of
biology to entertain it. Indeed, as we have seen, it is entirely
compatible with the theoretical formulations of contemporary
ethologists, sociobiologists, and psychiatrists. Precisely in order to
acquit himself of the charge of Lamarckism Jung eventually made
a clear distinction between what he termed the *archetype-as-such*
(similar to Kant's *das Ding-an-sich*) and the archetypal images,
ideas, and behaviours that the archetype-as-such gives rise to. It is
the *predisposition* to have certain experiences that is archetypal
and inherited, not the experience itself. The French molecular
biologist and Nobel Laureate Jacques Monod reached an identical
conclusion: 'Everything comes from experience, yet not from actual experience, reiterated by each individual with each generation,
but instead from experience accumulated by the entire ancestry of
the species in the course of its evolution.'

Thus, the Jungian archetype is no more scientifically disrepu-
table than the ethological IRM. Just as the behavioural repertoire of
each species is encoded in its central nervous system as innate
releasing mechanisms which are activated in the course of development by appropriate sign stimuli, so Jung conceived the programme for human life to be encoded in the collective unconscious
as a series of archetypal determinants which are actualized in
response to inner and outer events in the course of the life cycle.
There is nothing Lamarckian or unbiological in this conception.

Archetypes versus cultural transmission

Those who reject the archetypal hypothesis remain unimpressed
by the discovery of parallel themes in myths derived from different
parts of the world, maintaining that these can be explained just as
well by human migration and cultural diffusion as by an innate
predisposition. Jung sought to refute this interpretation by pointing
to the spontaneous occurrence of the same themes in the dreams,
hallucinations, and delusions of unsophisticated patients, who had
never previously encountered them in waking life: 'Typical
mythologems were observed among individuals to whom all

knowledge of this kind was absolutely out of the question,' he declared, concluding that 'we must be dealing with "auto-chthonous" revivals independent of all tradition, and, conse-quently, that "myth-forming" structural elements must be present in the unconscious psyche' (*CW* IX. i, para. 259). One example which Jung frequently quoted was that of a schizophrenic patient who told him that if he stared at the sun with half-closed eyes he would see that the sun had a phallus and that this organ was the origin of the wind. Years later Jung came across a Greek text describing an almost identical vision: 'And likewise the so-called tube, the origin of the ministering wind. For you will see hanging down from the disc of the sun something that looks like a tube . . .' (*CW* VIII, para. 318). The patient was a poorly educated man who could not, in any case, have seen the text, even if he could have understood it, since it was published after his admission to hos-pital, where no such literature was available.

Although this seems to have been Jung's favourite example to illustrate his thesis, it is not readily explicable as the result of archetypes operating in different individuals living in different places at different times in history. Much more persuasive exam-ples could have been given, such as the one we have just used, namely, the behaviour of generations of mothers and children as they live out the mother–child archetypal programme. To explain Jung's example it is necessary to postulate three archetypal objects (sun, phallus, and wind), an archetypal principle (that of masculine generativity), and an archetypal association between them (the sun's phallus generating the wind). Although such an association is statistically improbable, it is not impossible, as Jung's example would seem to demonstrate. But he could have found a more persuasive example to support his theory.

Essentially, the theory can be stated as a psychological law: *whenever a phenomenon is found to be characteristic of all hu-man communities, it is an expression of an archetype of the col-lective unconscious.* It is not possible to demonstrate that such universally apparent phenomena are exclusively due to archetypal determinants or entirely due to cultural diffusion, because in all probability both are involved. However, the likelihood is that there will be a strong *bias* for those phenomena which are archetypally determined to diffuse more readily and more lastingly than those that are not. Behavioural characteristics such as maternal bonding, dominance striving, sexual mating, and home building satisfy three critical biological criteria, namely, *universality, continuity*, and *evolutionary stability*, and as such are liable to be archetypally based, giving rise to typical psychological experiences as well as typical patterns of behaviour in all human communities wherever they exist.

The psychoid archetype and the *unus mundus*

The archetype possesses a fundamental duality: it is both a psychic structure and a neurological structure, both 'spirit' and 'matter', and Jung came to see it as the essential pre-condition of all psychophysical events: 'the archetypes are as it were the hidden foundations of the conscious mind, or, to use another comparison, the roots which the psyche has sunk not only in the earth in the narrower sense but in the world in general' (*CW* X, para. 53). He proposed that archetypal structures are not only fundamental to the existence and survival of all living organisms but that they are continuous with structures controlling the behaviour of inorganic matter as well. The archetype is not to be conceived, therefore, as merely a psychic entity but rather as 'the bridge to matter in general' (*CW* VIII, para. 420). This purely physical aspect of the archetype Jung sometimes referred to as the *psychoid* archetype, and it was an idea that greatly excited the physicist Wolfgang Pauli, who believed it made a major contribution to our ability to comprehend the principles on which the universe has been created.

Pauli's enthusiasm encouraged Jung to persevere in his attempts to penetrate that unitary reality which he, like the mystics of many religious traditions, believed to underlie all manifest phenomena. To describe this unitary dimension, Jung resurrected the ancient term *unus mundus*, or 'unitary world'—the eternal ground of all empirical being. He conceived archetypes to be the mediators of the *unus mundus*, responsible for organizing ideas and images in the psyche as well as for governing the fundamental principles of matter and energy in the physical world. Pauli argued that by conceiving archetypes in this way, Jung had discovered the 'missing link' between the physical events (which are the legitimate study of science) and the mind of the scientist who studies them.

41

In other words, the archetypes which order our perceptions and ideas are themselves the product of an objective order which transcends both the human mind and the external world. At this supreme point physical science, psychology, and theology all coalesce.

Synchronicity

With characteristic lack of caution, Jung extended these ideas into the realm of parapsychology, particularly the phenomenon of 'meaningful coincidence'—which he called *synchronicity*: 'A co-incidence in time of two or more causally unrelated events which have the same or similar meaning' (*CW* VIII, para. 849)—as when one dreams of the death of a distant friend the very same night that she dies. There can be no causal connection between the two events, yet we *experience* their conjunction as meaningful.

This 'acausal connecting principle', as Jung called it, is the basis of the ancient Chinese attitude to reality incorporated in the *I Ching* or *Book of Changes*—namely, that anything that happens is related to everything else that happens at the same time. Our Western world-view teaches that time is a purely abstract measure; but, if we are honest, it never *feels* as if it is. Indeed, the whole 'nostalgia industry' depends on our psychic awareness that time has a character all its own which colours events as they transpire. Jung intuitively felt this pointed to an acausal archetypal order at the root of all phenomena which is responsible for the meaningfulness implicit in the coincidence of associated physical and mental events.

Certainly, synchronistic happenings are occasionally part of the experience of most of us, and there is something inherently unsatisfactory about the way in which they are customarily dismissed in our culture as 'mere coincidence'. It is typical of Jung's approach that he was concerned with *all* experiences and that he took the irrational and apparently unconnected manifestations of human life as seriously as the rational and connected ones.

Implications

Whether or not one is persuaded by Jung's application of archetypal theory to the more esoteric areas of human experience, it is hard to deny that it is an idea with profound implications. If, as Jung believed, archetypes pre-condition all existence, then they must be manifest in the spiritual achievements of art, science, and religion as well as in the organization of organic and inorganic matter, and can provide a standpoint capable of transforming our understanding of all these phenomena. As far as psychology is concerned, the conception of the archetype as the common source of both behavioural and psychic events enables us to move beyond the intellectual quagmires of vitalism and epiphenomenalism which have so far hampered the progress of those seeking to explore the mysterious relationship between the body and the mind. Whatever else the archetypal hypothesis may achieve, it can at least provide a bridge between the science of mind and the science of behaviour.

3 The stages of life

The most profound influence of archetypes is in their regulation of the human life cycle. Jung maintained that as we mature we follow a natural sequence of steps which he describes in his essay 'The Stages of Life' (*CW* VIII, paras. 749–95). Each stage is mediated through a new set of archetypal imperatives which seek fulfilment in both our personality and our behaviour. Since the archetypes evolved to equip us for the hunter/gatherer existence in which our species has lived out 99 per cent of its existence, the archetypal programme equips us for a life which is not always in tune with the life of contemporary urban society. Essentially, the programme provides for being parented, exploring the environment, distinguishing familiar figures from strange, learning the language or dialect of one's community, acquiring a knowledge of its values, rules, and beliefs, playing in the peer group, meeting the challenges of puberty and adolescence, being initiated into the adult group, accomplishing courtship and marriage, and child-rearing, contributing to the economy through gathering and hunting, participating in religious rituals and ceremonials, assuming the responsibilities of advanced maturity, old age, and preparation for death. All these stages are apparent in all human communities known to anthropology and therefore obey the psychological law stated above on p. 40. As we have noted, the psychic nucleus responsible for co-ordinating this lifelong sequence Jung called the Self.

In addition to the Self, Jung postulated archetypal components which play specific roles in the psychic development and social adjustment of everyone. These include the *ego*, *persona*, *shadow*, *anima*, and *animus*. Jung considered these to be archetypal structures which are built into the personal psyche in the form of complexes during the course of development. Each is a psychic organ operating in accordance with the biological principles of adaptation, homeostasis, and growth. Though we make use of them and experience them in ways unique to ourselves, they nevertheless perform the same functions in all human beings everywhere. 'Ultimately,' wrote Jung, 'every individual life is at the same time the eternal life of the species' (*CW* XI, para. 146). In other words, we come into the world bearing with us an archetypal endowment which enables us to adapt to reality in the same way as our remote ancestors. The sum total of this endowment is incorporated in the Self and it is out of this matrix that the other psychic structures develop, and they remain under its guiding influence for the rest of life. We shall consider these now.

The Self

This is both architect and builder of the dynamic structure which supports our psychic existence throughout life. A capital S is used to distinguish between the 'self' of everyday usage (which refers to the ego or persona) and Jung's 'Self' which transcends the ego and inheres the age-old capacities of the species. Its goal is wholeness, the complete realization of the blueprint for human existence within the context of the life of the individual. *Individuation* is the *raison d'être* of the Self. Though it has evident biological goals, the Self also seeks fulfilment in the spiritual achievements of art and religion and in the inner life of the soul. Hence we can experience it as a profound mystery, a secret resource, or a manifestation of the God within. For this reason, it has been identified with the notion of deity in numerous cultures and finds symbolic expression in such universal configurations as the mandala. As a consequence, the Self came in Jung's view to provide the means of personal adjustment not only to the social environment but also to God, the cosmos, and the life of the spirit.

The ego

The ego complex emerges out of the Self in the course of early childhood development, rather as the moon is thought to have separated from the earth when the latter was in its early molten state. It remains linked to the Self by what Jung's followers have called the *ego–Self axis*, and it is on this axis that the stability of the personality depends. The ego is itself the centre of consciousness and it is what we refer to when we use the terms 'I' or 'me'. It

45

is responsible for our continuing sense of identity so that we still feel ourselves at 80 to be exactly the same person we were at 8. Jung never made a clear distinction between the terms 'ego' and 'consciousness', using them interchangeably and sometimes together as 'ego-consciousness'. As a result, he did not examine the more unconscious functions of the ego in defending consciousness against unwanted contents arising from the unconscious—those functions that Anna Freud described in her classic work *Mechanisms of Ego-Defence* (1946) (e.g. repression, denial, projection, rationalization, reaction-formation, to mention only the most familiar of them).

Although we experience the ego as the continuing centre of our existence it is, in fact, merely the Self's executive. 'For indeed our consciousness does not create itself—it wells up from unknown depths. In childhood it awakens gradually, and all through life it wakes each morning out of the depths of sleep from an unconscious condition. It is like a child that is born daily out of the primordial womb of the unconscious' (*CW* XI, para. 935). Again and again he stresses the dependency of ego-consciousness on the continuing vitality of the Self. 'The ego stands to the self as the moved to the mover, or as object to subject, because the determining factors which radiate out from the self surround the ego on all sides and are therefore supraordinate to it. The self, like the unconscious, is an *a priori* existent out of which the ego evolves' (*CW* XI, para. 391).

Put in terms of Jung's childhood experience the ego can be identified with his 'No. 1' personality and the Self with his 'No. 2'. In the first half of life it is essential to develop a strong and effective ego if one is to deal competently with the tasks of this stage—separating off from the parents, establishing oneself in a job or profession, marrying, providing a home for one's family, etc. Only in the second half of life does it become possible for the ego to recognize its subordinate status in relation to the Self—an indispensable stage in the progress of individuation. Then the ego begins to *confront* the Self and the Self the ego, and through the mediation of the *transcendent function* (which we will examine later) bring about the attainment of personality integration and higher consciousness.

The persona

Just as every building has a façade so every personality has a *persona* (literally a mask, as worn by actors in ancient Greece). Through the persona we codify ourselves in a form which we hope will prove acceptable to others. It has sometimes been referred to as the *social* archetype or the *conformity* archetype, for on it depends the success or failure of one's adaptation to society. There is always some element of pretence about the persona, for it is a kind of shop window in which we like to display our best wares; or one might think of it as a public relations expert employed by the ego to ensure that people will think well of us. 'One could say, with a little exaggeration, that the persona is that which in reality one is not, but which oneself as well as others think one is' (*CW* IX. i, para. 221).

The persona begins to form early in childhood out of a need to conform to the wishes and expectations of parents, peers, and teachers. Children quickly learn that certain attitudes and behaviours are acceptable and may be rewarded with approval while others are unacceptable and may result in punishment or the withdrawal of love. The tendency is to build acceptable traits into the persona and to keep unacceptable traits hidden or repressed. These socially undesirable aspects of the maturing personality are usually relegated to the personal unconscious, where they coalesce to form another complex, or part personality, that Jung called the shadow.

The shadow

Jung felt 'shadow' to be an appropriate term for this disowned subpersonality for there is inevitably something 'shady' about it, hidden away as it is in the dark lumber-room of the Freudian unconscious. Unwanted though it is, it persists as a powerful dynamic that we take with us wherever we go as a dark companion which dogs our steps—just like a shadow in fact. Much of the time we manage to ignore it, but it has an uncomfortable way of reminding us of its presence, particularly in our dreams.

In dreams the shadow tends to appear as a sinister or threatening

47

figure possessing the same sex as the dreamer, and is not infrequently a member of a different nation, colour, or race. There is usually something alien or hostile about it, which gives rise to powerful feelings of distrust, anger, or fear. This is why Jung felt justified in regarding the shadow as a *complex*—that is to say, a cluster of traits bound together by common affects—which, like all complexes, had an archetypal core, in this instance, the archetype of the Enemy, the Predator, or the Evil Stranger.

Of all archetypes the enemy is one of the most important and, potentially, the most deadly. Its influence becomes apparent during the first year of life. Just as the infant will show delight at being approached by its mother, so it will also show signs of wariness and withdrawal when approached by a stranger. By the second year, this xenophobic propensity has ripened into expressions of full-blown fear and hostility.

Both attachment and xenophobia are evidently the product of innate predispositions because they are apparent in all infants wherever they are born and under whatever circumstances they are brought up. Both are even apparent in children who have been blind and deaf from birth, who differentiate strangers from familiars by their smell. The biological significance of both patterns of behaviour is apparent from their manifestation by all social species: it is obviously a matter of survival to be able to distinguish between friend and foe from the earliest possible age.

The archetype of the enemy is actualized in the personal psyche as the shadow complex through growing up in a human social environment. There are two important sources of the complex: (1) cultural indoctrination, and (2) familial repression.

The cultural source includes all that one has been taught politically about out-groups considered to be hostile to one's in-group (i.e. nation, tribe, or band) and theologically about the concept of evil (in our culture, Satan, the Devil, Hell). Inevitably, the shadow comes to possess qualities opposite to those of the persona, the shadow compensating, as it were, for the superficial pretensions of the persona, the persona balancing the antisocial characteristics of the shadow. The coexistence of these two sharply contrasting personalities within the same individual is as apparent in literature as in life: Dorian Gray, the handsome, witty, man-about-town, keeps his portrait hidden where no one can see it, for it bears all the features of his vicious secret life; Dr Jekyll and Mr Hyde are the same man, by turns respectable physician and monstrous ogre; the popular TV personality with the compassionate manner and caring smile can be a hysterical termagant at home with her family.

To some extent we all resemble Dorian Gray in keeping our shadow out of sight, not as an act of will but as an act of submission to that inner authority which Freud called the *super-ego* and Jung called the *moral complex*. In the light of Bowlby's work, it seems that the impetus to develop this inner watch-dog is not, as Freud believed, a fear of being castrated by the father as a reprisal for entertaining incestuous desires, but rather a fear of being *abandoned* by the mother for being unacceptable. The dread prospect of being rejected on account of some 'bad' aspect of the Self seems to be at the bottom of all feelings of guilt, all desire for punishment, and all longings for atonement and reconciliation. The moral complex forms on the basis of an archetypal imperative to learn and maintain the values of the culture into which we happen to have been born. If no such imperative existed, anarchy would be the natural human condition: we should all be psychopaths, incapable of co-operation or mutual trust, and the species could not conceivably exist.

However, the acquisition of a moral complex imposes severe restraints on the Self, much of which is necessarily relegated to the shadow, where it is experienced—when it is experienced—as a threat. To defend ourselves from this threat, and to sustain our peace of mind, we make use of a variety of ego-defence mechanisms, particularly *repression*, *denial*, and *projection*. Not only do we repress the shadow in the personal unconscious, but we deny its existence in ourselves, and project it out on to others. This is done quite unconsciously: we are not aware that we do it. It is an act of ego-preservation which enables us to deny our own 'badness' and to attribute it to others, whom we then hold responsible for it. It explains the ubiquitous practice of *scapegoating* and underlies all kinds of prejudice against people belonging to identifiable groups other than our own. Shadow projection is also involved in the psychiatric symptom of paranoia, when one's own hostile, persecutory feelings are disowned and projected on to others, who are then experienced as being hostile and persecutory towards oneself.

Shadow projection can function, therefore, as a major threat to both social and international peace, for it enables us to turn those whom we perceive as enemies into devils or vermin that it is legitimate to hate, attack, or exterminate. Unscrupulous leaders can manipulate this mechanism in whole populations. Adolf Hitler, for example, repeatedly described the Jews as *Untermenschen* (subhumans) and through the skilful use of propaganda was able to induce enough Germans to project their shadow on to them as to make the holocaust possible. The same mechanism is involved in all pogroms, all 'ethnic cleansing', and all wars.

The most demanding part of a Jungian analysis occurs when the *analysand* (the person undergoing analysis) begins to confront his own shadow. That this should be difficult is not surprising since the whole shadow complex is tinged with feelings of guilt and unworthiness, and with fears of rejection should its true nature be discovered or exposed. However painful the process may be, it is necessary to persevere because much Self potential and instinctive energy is locked away in the shadow and therefore unavailable to the total personality. People suffering from this inner state of Self-division commonly complain of feeling flat and listless, and that life has become meaningless for them. Analytic success in making the shadow conscious and coming to terms with its contents results, after the initial struggle, in a sense of greater vitality, of feeling more vigorous, more creative, and more whole. To own one's shadow is to become responsible for it, so that one's morality is less blind and less compulsive, and ethical choices become possible. Shadow consciousness is important not only for personal development, therefore, but as a basis for greater social harmony and international understanding.

Sex and gender

While Jung acknowledged that environmental factors exert an enormous influence over a person's psychological development, he nevertheless maintained that these influences act by bringing out the 'subjective aptitudes' with which all children are born. He held this to be as true of gender awareness as it is of development of the persona, the shadow, or the psychological type. The specious idea that gender differences are due entirely to culture, and have nothing to do with biological or archetypal predispositions, still enjoys wide currency in our society, yet it rests on the discredited *tabula rasa* theory of human development and is at variance with the overwhelming mass of anthropological and scientific evidence.

Sexual differentiation begins approximately six weeks after conception, when in male children the gonads are formed and begin to manufacture male hormone, which has a profound effect on the future development of the embryo. In the female, on the other hand, the ovaries are not formed until the sixth month, by which time the greater size, weight, and muscular strength of the male is already established. This is the biological basis of the sexual dimorphism apparent in the great majority of societies known to anthropology, where child-rearing is almost invariably the responsibility of women, and hunting and warfare the responsibility of men. These differences have less to do with cultural 'stereotypes' than some fashionable contemporary notions would have us believe. While it is true that at all ages males and females have far more in common than they have differences between them, there can be no doubt that some differences exist which have their roots in the biology of our species. Jung was quite clear about this. Again and again, he refers to the masculine and the feminine as two great archetypal principles, coexisting as equal and complementary parts of a balanced cosmic system, as expressed in the interplay of *yin* and *yang* in Taoist philosophy. These archetypal principles provide the foundations on which masculine and feminine stereotypes begin to do their work, providing an awareness of gender. Gender is the psychic recognition and social expression of the sex to which nature has assigned us, and a child's awareness of its gender is established by as early as eighteen months of age.

Initially, the mother functions as a 'carrier' of the Self, in the sense that the child's Self is unconsciously *projected* on to the mother in a *participation mystique* (a term which Jung borrowed from the anthropologist Lévy-Brühl to denote a relationship in which both partners are so intensely identified with one another as to be unaware of their separate existence). This is true of both boys

and girls, and gender awareness has to be superimposed on this
original sense of oneness with the mother. For a girl this presents
no problem: her gender consciousness is based on *shared* identity
with her mother. But for the boy, a transformation has to be
achieved to an awareness of an identity based on *difference* from
the mother. At this point, the presence of a father-figure can prove
crucial, enabling the boy to move from a self-concept based on
mother identity to one based on identification-with-father. For the
girl, the father's presence is no less important, for it heightens her
sense of being female in contrast to the essential 'otherness' of the
male, and so profoundly influences how she *experiences* her
femininity in relation to men.

In mythology the dawning of consciousness is symbolized by the
separation of the world parents, Father Heaven from Mother Earth,
and the creation of light out of darkness. Originally, the sky lay flat
upon the earth, and so the world parents remained until a hero got
between them and gave the sky such an enormous shove that it
flew up into the firmament and has remained there ever since. This
momentous event was followed by the coming of light—the
symbol of consciousness and 'illumination'.

As the parent–child relationship matures within the traditional
family setting, there is a growing awareness on the part of the child
that father-love differs from mother-love: the father's love is *con-
tingent* love (i.e. it is conditional upon the adoption of certain
values, standards, and modes of conduct) while the mother's love is
largely *unconditional* (i.e. it is usually sufficient for her that her
child *exists*). This distinction accords with the phenomenological
differences between the father and mother archetypes as represented in myths, religions, and fairy-tales. While the mother archetype finds universal expression as Mother Nature, Goddess of
Fertility, Womb of Life, and Dispenser of Nourishment, the father
archetype is personified as Ruler, Elder, King, and Lawgiver. The
mother is abundantly endowed with *Eros*, the principle of love,
intimacy, and relatedness, while the father is the living embodiment of *Logos*, the principle of reason, judgement, and discrimina-
tion. His word is law. Jung wrote:

The archetype of the mother is the most immediate one for the child. But
with the development of consciousness, the father also enters the field of

vision, and activates an archetype whose nature is in many respects opposed to that of the mother. Just as the mother archetype corresponds to the Chinese *yin*, so the father archetype corresponds to the *yang*. It determines our relation to man, to the law and the state, to reason and the spirit and the dynamism of nature. (*CW* X, para. 65)

Gender consciousness and an awareness of the characteristics of the opposite sex, having been established in relation to the parents, are refined through interaction with the peer group, especially in play. The roles children adopt in play are, of course, culturally related, being based on mimicry of the parents and other significant adults in the community. But, as evidence from widely differing societies indicates, these cultural influences proceed on the basis of an archetypal design. Virtually everywhere, it appears that girls tend to be more nurturant and affiliative than boys in that they are more prone to seek the proximity of others and to show pleasure in doing so. Boys, on the other hand, are less interested in social interaction for its own sake and tend to prefer some form of physical activity, such as running, chasing, and playing with large, movable toys. They also tend to be more rowdy and aggressive and less amenable to control by adults and their peers.

Anima and animus

Just as gender is experienced as an affirmation of the archetypal principle appropriate to one's sex, so relations with the other sex rest on an archetypal foundation. Of all the archetypal systems enabling us to adapt to the typical circumstances of human life, that involved in relating to the opposite sex is the most crucial. Jung called this contrasexual archetype the *animus* in women and the *anima* in men. As the feminine aspect of man and the masculine aspect of woman, they function as a pair of opposites (the *syzygy*) in the unconscious of both, profoundly influencing the relations of all men and women with each other.

Jung also found that in practice both anima and animus act in dreams and in the imagination as mediators of the unconscious to the ego, so providing a means for inner as well as outer adaptation. He described them as 'soul-images' and the 'not-I', for they are experienced as something mysterious and numinous, possessing great power. The more unconscious the anima or animus, the more likely it is to be projected—the psychodynamic process responsible for the experience of 'falling in love'. For this reason, Jung called the contrasexual complex the 'projection-making factor'.

'Every man carries within him the eternal image of the woman, not the image of this or that woman, but a definite feminine image. This image is fundamentally unconscious, an hereditary factor of primordial origin . . .' (*CW* XVII, para. 338). 'Woman is compensated by a masculine element and therefore her unconscious has, so to speak, a masculine imprint . . . and accordingly I have called the projection-making factor in women the animus . . . The animus corresponds to the paternal Logos just as the anima corresponds to the maternal Eros' (*CW* IX. ii, para. 28).

As with the shadow, the contrasexual complex possesses qualities opposite to those manifested in the persona, for, even in our egalitarian times, boys are expected to be boys and girls to be girls. Thus, the more a man is incapable of accepting his shadow and the feminine qualities in himself the more he is identified with his persona. Indeed, Jung even goes so far as to declare that 'the character of the anima can be deduced from that of the persona' because 'everything that should normally be in the outer attitude, but is conspicuously absent, will invariably be found in the inner attitude. This is a fundamental rule . . .' (*CW* VI, para. 806).

A self-regulating system

This fundamental rule is the *homeostatic* rule of self-regulation, which Jung borrowed from biology and applied to human psychology. Homeostasis is the means by which all organic systems keep themselves in a state of balance, despite changes in the environment. In fact, homeostatic regulation can be observed at all levels of existence, from molecules to communities, in living as well as non-living systems, and our whole planet is conceivable as one vast homeostatic system. Because the psyche evolved in the context of the world, Jung held that the laws which prevail in the cosmos must also prevail in the psyche. He therefore felt justified in viewing the psyche as a self-regulating system which strives perpetually to maintain a balance between opposing propensities, while, at the same time, seeking its own growth and development.

The psyche is a self-regulating system that maintains its equilibrium just as the body does. Every process that goes too far immediately and inevitably calls forth compensations, and without these there would be neither a normal metabolism nor a normal psyche. In this sense we can take the theory of compensation as a basic law of psychic behaviour. Too little on one side results in too much on the other. Similarly, the relation between conscious and unconscious is compensatory. (*CW* XVI, para. 330)

The principle of compensation is the key concept of Jungian psychodynamics, in that it is central to Jung's understanding of how the psyche adapts and develops in the course of the life cycle.

A programme for life

Jung's approach to developmental psychology was so different from that prevailing throughout his lifetime that it marked him out in the eyes of many as a maverick. In the orthodox behaviourist view the human organism was a mere response system which reacted to outer stimuli to build up a repertoire of behaviours through conditioning and learning. Jung, on the contrary, held that human beings were born with an elaborate programme for life which presupposed the natural life cycle of humanity and was incorporated in the Self. As he wrote:

Behind a man's actions there stands neither public opinion nor the moral code, but the personality of which he is still unconscious. Just as a man still is what he always was, so he already is what he will become. The conscious mind does not embrace the totality of a man, for this totality consists only partly of his conscious contents . . . In this totality the conscious mind is contained like a smaller circle within a larger one. (*CW* XI, para. 390)

As one passes from one stage of the life cycle to the next, new and appropriate aspects of the Self become active and demand expression, and Jung believed that this inner programme imparted to the second half of life a quality quite different from the first. The primary concerns of the first half are biological and social, while those of the second are cultural and spiritual. 'Man has two aims,' he wrote. 'The first is the natural aim, the begetting of children and the business of protecting the brood; to this belongs the acquisition of money and social position.' Only when this aim has been achieved does the new aim—'the cultural aim'—become feasible (*CW* VII, para. 114).

Transition from one stage of the life cycle to the next is a time of potential crisis for everyone and it was in order to assist the individual through these critical period that *rites of passage* evolved in primitive societies. These rites—particularly puberty initiation rites, rites of incorporation into the hunter, warrior, or shamanic role, marriage rites, rites on the birth of children and the death of relations—possessed great value because they provided public affirmation of the fact that a significant transition had occurred and, through the powerful symbolism of the ritual, activated archetypal components in the collective unconscious appropriate to the life stage that had been reached: this archetypal potential was then incorporated in the personal psyche of the initiate.

Archetypal expectations

Maturation is to be conceived, therefore, as proceeding through an innate sequence of archetypal *expectations*, namely, that the environment will provide the following: sufficient *nourishment*, *warmth*, and *protection* from predators and enemies to guarantee physical survival, a *family* consisting of mother, father, and peers; sufficient *space for exploration and play*; a *community* to supply language, myth, religion, ritual, values, stories, initiation, and, eventually, a *mate*; and an *economic* role and/or *vocational status*.

Although these archetypal requirements are the same for everyone, each culture will succeed (or fail) in meeting them in its own way and every individual's experience of living through the sequence will be unique. Thus, the actual qualities of the parents will have a profound influence on a child's development, for they will determine the quality and content of the mother and father complexes in the child's personal psyche, which in turn provide the foundations on which the mature personality is built. However, these complexes are never simple 'video clips' of the actual parents: they are parental *imagos*, the products of a continuous interaction between the personal parents in the environment and the archetypal parents in the collective unconscious. The crucial criterion is that the actual parents should be 'good enough' to actualize the parental archetypes, namely, that they should be sufficiently present (to satisfy the law of *contiguity*) and sufficiently appropriate in their care-giving (to satisfy the law of *similarity*) to approximate to the child's archetypal expectations. Where the parents are not 'good enough' the rest of the programme for life may be distorted and later stages in the archetypal sequence may fail to be realized. Thus, the boy whose father was inadequate or absent may fail to actualize his masculine potential sufficiently to establish the social or vocational role his talents equip him for, or he may be unable to sustain a relationship with a member of the opposite sex long enough for him to become an adequate husband or father himself.

Rites of passage

The archetypal tasks of childhood and adolescence for the male are symbolized in the hero myths which are found in all parts of the world. These tell how the hero leaves home and is subjected to a number of tests and trials, culminating in the 'supreme ordeal' of a fight with a dragon or a sea monster. The hero's triumph is rewarded with the 'treasure hard to attain', i.e. the throne of a kingdom and a beautiful princess as a bride. So it is in actuality: to embark on the adventure of life, a boy has to free himself of his bonds to home, parents, and siblings, survive the ordeals of initiation (which virtually all traditional societies imposed), and win a place for himself in the world (the kingdom). To achieve all this and to win a bride, he must overcome the power of the mother complex still operative in his unconscious (the fight with the dragon). This amounts to a second parturition from the mother, a final severing of the psychic umbilical cord (victory over the dragon-monster often involves the hero being swallowed into its belly from which he cuts his way out in a kind of auto-Caesarian section: as a result, he 'dies' as his mother's son and is 'reborn' as a man worthy of the princess and the kingdom). The ritual of masculine initiation at puberty facilitates this necessary transition. Failure to pass the ordeals of initiation or to overcome the monster, signifies failure to get free of the mother: then the princess (the anima) is never liberated from the monster's clutches. She remains trapped and inert in the unconscious in the custody of the mother complex.

In girls, the transition to womanhood is more readily accomplished since feminine gender consciousness does not demand a radical shift of identification from mother's world to father's world as it does in boys. As a result, female initiation, where it occurs, is (with the exception of the culturally rare and appalling rite of female circumcision) a less demanding and protracted process than for boys, consisting essentially of a ceremonial recognition that a young woman has now entered the reproductive phase of her life. It is as if the ritual were designed to heighten her introverted awareness of herself as a woman *creative on the plane of life itself*, with access to a sacred realm of experience that man can never know. (Man himself recognizes this and is filled with awe: 'The anima', wrote Jung, 'is the *archetype of life itself*' (*CW* IX. i, para. 66); Jung's italics.)

In many cultures there are no female initiation rites, and the task of bringing this new feminine consciousness into being falls to the initiated male. Hence the myths and fairy-tales in which the heroine lies sleeping till a prince comes to awaken her with a kiss (awakening his own anima in the process). She is the Sleeping Beauty surrounded by a thicket, or the slumbering Brünnhilde awaiting the arrival of her Siegfried within the circle of Wotan's fire.

Although our culture no longer provides rites of initiation, there persists in all of us, regardless of gender, *an archetypal need to be initiated*. We can deduce this from the dreams of patients in analysis which become rich in initiatory symbolism at critical periods of their lives—e.g. at puberty, betrothal, marriage, child-birth, at divorce or separation, at the death of a parent or spouse. Attainment of a new stage of life seems to demand that symbols of initiation must be experienced. If society fails to provide them, then the Self compensates for this deficiency by producing them in dreams.

The dynamics of progress

For all young people growth is a hard journey out of the familiar past into an unknown future, and there are times when everyone feels daunted by the precarious uncertainty of the path. Sometimes its challenges may appear so overwhelming that individuals break down, give up, or regress to a previous stage of development, returning to the mother in her archetypal aspect of nurturer and container. In the circumstances, this may well be an appropriate strategy, a *reculer pour mieux sauter* to recover enough strength and determination to encounter the ordeals that lie ahead.

An inherent conflict is apparent at this stage: the archetypal programme decrees that we must separate from the mother and grow away from her but, at the same time, hold on to the love and security she represents: 'Whoever sunders himself from the mother longs to get back to the mother. This longing can easily turn into a consuming passion which threatens all that has been won' (*CW* V, para. 352). It was this threat that rites of passage were meant to overcome, for, as Jung discovered in his confrontation with the unconscious, a dual dynamic is at work in all psychic development. On the one hand, we are driven outwards and onwards into the future; on the other, we are pulled inwards and backwards to the past. Development is never a simple, linear progress: it is a spiral with progressive ascents and regressive descents. But from his own experience, Jung learned that regression can act in the service of growth and that psychiatric illness may represent an effort on the part of the psyche to heal itself.

The period from adolescence to early adulthood is the time when people are most highly motivated to look after 'No. 1', pouring all their energies into job, marriage, home, and children. It is a time of rapid, if one-sided, development, when few people have much time to devote to their inner life. For this reason, Jung maintained that a psychological commitment to the path of individuation was hardly appropriate to this stage. On the contrary, this is the time to pay one's dues to society in order to purchase the right to individuate, which then becomes the task of the second half of life.

Love and marriage

In most people the capacity to relate to the opposite sex matures during adolescence and early adulthood to the point where marriage becomes both possible and desired, should circumstances allow. The experience of 'falling in love' occurs, as we have seen, when one meets a woman or man who, rightly or wrongly, appears to be the living embodiment of one's anima or animus. This profoundly moving experience is an example of what it means to be 'taken over' by the power of an autonomous complex.

Every archetype, once activated, seeks its own fulfilment in life. This is specially true of the animus and anima, for their quest for completion is rendered more imperative by the nagging insistence of sexual desire. Bonding with a partner is more than just a matter of unconscious projection. If the bond is to last long enough for children to be reared, then it has to be sustained by continuing sexual interest, the insistence of the law, and the recognition by each partner of the other as a real person, with qualities over and beyond those that have been projected. Failure to forgive a spouse for *not* living up to his anima or her animus fantasies can lead to heartache, recrimination, and divorce.

Jung was very aware of this from his own experience of marriage. In his essay 'Marriage as a Psychological Relationship', published in 1925, he argues that a marriage can only be a true relationship if it transcends blind mutual animus/anima projections and if both partners become *conscious* of each other's psychic reality. Otherwise it remains a 'medieval marriage', ruled by custom and illusion, a mere *participation mystique* ('one heart and one soul'). In present circumstances, marriage has to be a more conscious, less stereotyped institution, even if this entails feelings of disillusionment as the contrasexual fantasies are withdrawn, and results in an increased incidence of separation and divorce. 'There is no birth of consciousness without pain' (*CW* XVII, para. 331).

If, however, the union survives, then it can become what has been called an 'individuation marriage' (Guggenbühl-Craig, *Marriage, Dead or Alive?* Zürich: Spring Publications, 1977) enabling both personalities to grow through a richer understanding of each other, their marriage, and themselves. 'This is what happens very frequently about the midday of life,' says Jung, 'and in this wise our miraculous human nature enforces a transition that leads from the first half of life to the second. It is a metamorphosis from a state in which man is only a tool of instinctive nature to another in which he is no longer a tool, but himself: a transformation of nature into culture, of instinct into spirit' (*CW* XVII, para. 335).

Jung's views on same-sex love also drew on his animus/anima concepts. The homosexual is one who, in the course of growing up, has identified more closely with the parent of the opposite sex while the same sex potential has remained relatively unconscious and unactualized. As a result, the essential polarity of sexual attraction, the desire for union with the 'unknown other', is experienced in relation to members of the same sex who appear to have those desirable qualities which are felt to be lacking.

Thus, when male homosexuals come into analysis it is often because they have been unable to find what they are questing for, namely, the love partner who is perceived as the embodiment of their own unactualized masculine potential. Analysis can help to make the psychological significance of this quest conscious and pave the way for an 'individuation relationship' with another man, in which each helps the other to find what he has been questing for. Similar considerations apply to the analysis of homosexual women.

These and other implications of Jungian theory for gay psychology are well presented in *Jung, Jungians and Homosexuality* by Robert H. Hopcke (Boston: Shambhala, 1989).

The stroke of noon

Jung's comparison of mid-life with midday is drawn from his metaphor of life as the diurnal course of the sun:

In the morning it rises from the nocturnal sea of unconsciousness and looks upon the wide, bright world which lies before it in an expanse that steadily widens the higher it climbs in the firmament. In this extension of its field of action caused by its own rising, the sun will discover its own significance; it will see the attainment of the greatest possible height, and the widest possible dissemination of its blessings, as its goal. In this conviction the sun pursues its course to the unforeseen zenith—unforeseen, because its career is unique and individual, and the culminating point could not be calculated in advance. At the stroke of noon the descent begins. And the descent means the reversal of all the ideals and values that were cherished in the morning. The sun falls into contradiction with itself. It is as though it should draw in its rays instead of emitting them. Light and warmth decline and are at last extinguished ... (*CW* VIII, para. 778)

At the middle of life an *enantiodromia* occurs, carrying with it terse intimations of mortality. For many this is a time of crisis, of

Jung

self-doubt, and inner questioning. 'What exactly have I achieved with my life?' 'What am I to do with the rest of it?' 'What is there to look forward to but old age, infirmity, and death?' 'The wine has fermented and begins to settle and clear,' comments Jung. '. . . instead of looking forward one looks backward . . . one begins to take stock, to see how one's life has developed up to this point' (*CW* XVII, para. 331*a*). The period from 35 to 45 is one of raised rates of depression, divorce, and suicide. Somewhat later women have to confront the additional problems of menopause. However, as Jung discovered for himself, the mid-life crisis, though traumatic, is also an opportunity to become more conscious and to grow.

Success in the first half of life usually requires channelling one's energies single-mindedly in a specific direction. This results in development of a relatively narrow, 'one-sided' personality and a failure to actualize much Self potential which remains dormant in the unconscious. As Jung emphasized, *'Personality need not imply consciousness. It can just as easily be dormant or dreaming'* (*CW* IX. i, para. 508; Jung's italics). The crisis of mid-life can serve to 'wake up' this dreaming, undiscovered Self and the rest of life can provide the opportunity for its development. With this realization the real work of individuation can begin, for individuation is a process of bringing to conscious awareness the developmental process unfolding within oneself.

The individuation of the Self

Philosophers have shown interest in the *principium individuationis* since Aristotle, but only a handful of developmental psychologists have studied the phenomenon in the present century, using such terms for it as 'self-realization' or 'self-actualization'. Jung's concept went further, however, because he viewed individuation as a biological principle evident in all living organisms and not restricted to human beings. 'Individuation', he wrote, 'is an expression of that biological process—simple or complicated as the case may be—by which every living thing becomes what it was destined to become from the beginning' (*CW* XI, para. 144). As with the archetypes themselves, he eventually came to believe that individuation was at work in inorganic matter as well—as when a crystal forms out of a hidden configuration within its pre-existent liquor.

But as a psychologist what fascinated him was what he saw as the highest achievement of the individuation principle—the human psyche in its fullest possible development. It is a creative act of Self-completion: a progressive integration of the unconscious, timeless Self (which Jung sometimes referred to as 'the two million-year-old man that is in all of us') with the time-bound personality of the contemporary man or woman. How does this extraordinary fusion occur? The answer is that it occurs in our sleep and that the process is immeasurably assisted if we record our dreams, reflect on them, and work on them.

Describing the work of analysis, Jung wrote: 'Together the patient and I address ourselves to the two million-year-old man that is in all of us. In the last analysis, most of our difficulties come from losing contact with our instincts, with the age-old unforgotten wisdom stored up in us. And where do we make contact with this old man in us? In our dreams' (*Psychological Reflections*, 76).

As will be described in Chapter 5, Jung proposed that dreams play an indispensable role in psychic homeostasis, in that they promote adaptation to the demands of life by compensating the one-sided limitations of consciousness. Repeated night after night, and year after year, this compensatory activity makes recurrent contributions to the individuation process, as becomes readily apparent when one examines a long series of dreams from the same person.

Remembering dreams, writing them down, and analysing them enhances this homeostatic function. But dreams continue to do their work whether we remember them or not. After all, the great majority of dreams occur without anyone being consciously aware of them, yet they must have a crucial purpose since virtually all animals dream, and dreaming brains have been around for 135 million years. It would be an extraordinary waste of nature's time if dreams did not contribute in some vitally important way to survival. As it turns out, both ethology and Jungian psychology share a common view of this fascinating phenomenon, though few ethologists (and indeed few Jungians) are aware of the fact. In the ethological view, dreams perform the task of integrating the daily experience of an animal with the programme for life laid down in the genome (the total genetic constitution) of the species. Dreams promote the animal's competence to survive and provide the means by which the basic patterns of the life cycle are realized. This is individuation proceeding at the natural, organic level.

The kind of individuation that was the centre of Jung's concern was the process consciously lived out by men and women actively seeking to become as complete an incarnation of humanity as it was in them to be. Circumstances inevitably impose constraints on personal development, and just as no mother can hope to embody the totality of the mother archetype so no individual can ever hope to incorporate the whole potential of the collective unconscious. However fortunate our upbringing may have been, few of us by middle age can hope to be any more than a 'good enough' version of the Self. One can, nevertheless, follow the Apollonian advice to 'know thyself', heed Pindar's dictum 'Become what thou art', and learn from Plato and Aristotle to discover one's 'true self'—to make explicit what implicitly one already is. In Jungian terms this means overcoming the divisions imposed by the parental and cultural milieu, to divest oneself of 'the false wrappings of the persona' (*CW* VII, para. 269), abandon one's ego-defences, and, rather than projecting one's shadow on to others, strive to know it and acknowledge it as part of one's inner life, come to terms with the contrasexual personality living within the personal psyche, and attempt to bring to conscious fulfilment the supreme intentions of the Self. Complete achievement of these objectives within the compass of one individual lifetime is never possible, of course, but that is not the point. 'The goal is important only as an idea,' wrote Jung; 'the essential thing is the *opus* which leads to the goal: *that* is the goal of a lifetime' (*CW* XVI, para. 400).

To commit oneself to the *opus* is to live fruitfully into old age while discharging the spiritual obligations of late maturity. 'A human being would certainly not grow to be seventy or eighty years old if this longevity had no meaning for the species. The afternoon of life must have a significance of its own and cannot be merely a pitiful appendage of life's morning' (*CW* VIII, para. 787).

To use these years to become as complete a human being as we can within the limitations of our culture is to contribute to the well-being of society as much as to the personal fulfilment of our lives. Well individuated older people are, and always have been, the repositories of wisdom, for they have had time to reflect, to integrate all they have learned with a lifetime of experience. However well educated the young may be, 'book learning' can never rival the inspiration to be gained from someone who *knows* and has *lived*. To individuate is to realize one's personal existence as a unique expression of humanity and, within the frail vessel of one's little psychic world, to distil the essence of creation. In this microcosmic experiment the great cosmos becomes conscious of itself.

4 Psychological types

Jung was concerned with both the universal and the particular in human life. Psychology had to define what psychic structures and functions all people shared in common and then describe how these came to be assembled in the unique combination that makes up the individual personality. *Psychological Types* (*CW* VI), published in 1921, was his first attempt to achieve this dual purpose.

It is a reasonable assumption that all people have broadly the same psychological equipment with which to perceive what is happening outside and inside themselves, to formulate ideas about it, and to determine how to respond to events as they occur. Where people differ is in the way that each of them typically makes use of the equipment; and this typical mode of apperception and responsiveness is what is meant in psychology by their 'type'.

The questions which must exercise the ingenuity of any psychologist attempting to devise a typology are (1) what are the essential components of the equipment, and (2) how do people differ in using these components to form their habitual mode of adaptation to reality? Jung's answers to these questions were (1) that the equipment consists of four psychological *functions*, which he named *sensation*, *thinking*, *feeling*, and *intuition*, all of which are available a priori to everybody, and (2) that individuals differ in regard to which of the four functions they use for preference.

A further distinction between people depends on whether they habitually place greater emphasis on the importance of outer objective events or inner subjective ones (i.e. whether their *attitude* to reality is characteristically *extraverted* or *introverted*).

The four functions

In *Psychological Types* Jung describes the different characteristics of the four functions in great detail, but he summed up this information very succinctly in *Man and his Symbols*, published two years after his death: 'These four functional types correspond to the obvious means by which consciousness obtains its orientation to experience. *Sensation* (i.e., sense perception) tells us that something exists; *thinking* tells you what it is; *feeling* tells you whether it is agreeable or not; and *intuition* tells you whence it comes and where it is going' (*Man and his Symbols*, 61).

Jung considered thinking and feeling to be *rational* functions and sensation and intuition to be *irrational* functions. Few people find it hard to agree that thinking, to be effective, needs to be logical and rational; but many have difficulty in conceiving feeling as a rational process. This, says Jung, is because they confuse feeling with *emotion* or *affect*. Feeling, as he used the term, can certainly give rise to emotions but only when the feeling is powerful enough to trigger biochemical or neurological changes in the body; its normal use is to make value-judgements about inner or outer events to determine whether they are pleasant or unpleasant, beautiful or ugly, desirable or undesirable, good or bad, etc. This requires evaluative reflection in the light of past experience and is, therefore, in Jung's view, a rational process. Confusion over this issue is reduced if one thinks of Jung's feeling function as a judgemental process concerned with values: *evaluating* function might be a more appropriate term.

As a psychological function, sensation is the means by which we process in consciousness the evidence of our senses and build up percepts of our world. Intuition is the means by which we make inferences about the possibilities inherent in a situation presented to our awareness at any given moment. To describe these two functions as 'irrational', as Jung does, is unhelpful because it gives the impression that he regarded them as in some way pathological or 'mad'. By 'irrational' he wished to imply that they functioned in a way that had nothing to do with reason. 'Non-rational' would be a better term.

The two attitudes

The way in which each function manifests in the psychology of the individual depends on the characteristic *attitude* adopted by him or her. Whereas the *extravert* is oriented primarily to events in the outer world, the *introvert* is primarily concerned with the inner world. Typically, the extravert has 'an outgoing, candid and accommodating nature that adapts easily to a given situation, quickly forms attachments, and, setting aside any possible misgivings, will often venture forth with careless confidence into unknown situations'. The introvert, on the other hand, has 'a hesitant, reflective, retiring nature that keeps itself to itself, shrinks from objects, is always slightly on the defensive and prefers to hide behind mistrustful scrutiny' (*CW* VII, para. 43).

A pub brawl

An example will help to clarify what Jung meant by these different functions and attitudes. Let us imagine that four people, a sensation type, a thinking type, a feeling type, and an intuitive type, witness the following scene:

Two men come staggering out of a bar. They are shouting and swearing at one another. There is a struggle. One of them falls to the ground and bangs his head on the pavement.

Each witness will respond to these events in a manner typical of his type. We will take each of them in turn.

The sensation type will give the clearest account of what happened. He will have noted the height, build, and general appearance of the two men: one was fat, middle-aged, and bald and had a scar over his left eye; the other younger, fair-haired, more athletic, and had a moustache. Both were dressed casually in T-shirts, jeans, and trainers. It was the fat one who fell and it was his right temple that struck the kerb. There was a crack on impact, etc.

The thinking type interprets the events as they happen, working out what it all means. The two men come staggering out of the bar, so evidently they have been drinking. They are shouting and swearing at one another, so they are having a disagreement. A struggle ensues, so they must feel strongly enough to become physically violent about it. One falls to the ground, so he must be the weaker (or drunker) of the two. The latter cracks his head, so he may be concussed and in need of medical attention, etc.

The feeling type responds to each event in the scene with value-judgements: 'What a sordid episode!' 'What thoroughly objectionable people!' 'That is clearly a bar frequented by louts and not a place to go to if one wants a quiet chat with a friend.' 'The one on the ground may have hurt himself, but it serves him right!' etc.

The intuitive type 'sees' the whole story: they are football hooligans who support opposing teams. Disgusted by their bad language, the landlord told them to clear off, and this inflamed them to violence. The man who cracked his head is accident prone, and this is just another incident in a lifetime of misfortune. He has fractured his skull and a clot will form on his brain requiring surgery. He will be off work for weeks and his long-suffering wife will once again have to struggle to make ends meet. This is what happens to people from a poor cultural background, who have nothing else to live for but football and drink. Things like this will go on happening and get much worse because we do nothing to change society or improve the educational system, etc.

Similar observations, thoughts, value-judgements, and intuitions to those just described are available to anyone who chanced to witness this episode, but Jung's point is that each of us will characteristically tend to emphasize one functional mode in monitoring the events rather than the other three. Habitual use of this mode is what determines one's functional type. Moreover, how one responds to the episode will also be determined by one's characteristic attitude, an extravert being more likely to intervene, render first aid, drag the assailant off, call for an ambulance, etc., while the introvert will be more prone to observe, record, and inwardly reflect on what has occurred, preferring to leave it to someone else (i.e. an extravert) or an official whose job it is to do something about it.

Eight psychological types

Out of the two *attitude* types and the four *functional* types it becomes theoretically possible to describe eight psychological types: the extraverted sensation type, the introverted sensation type, the extraverted thinking type, the introverted thinking type, and so on. Jung observed that it is rare for people to make exclusive use of one function: they tend to develop two functions, usually one *rational* function and one *irrational* function; one of these becomes the *primary* or *superior* function and the other an *auxiliary* function.

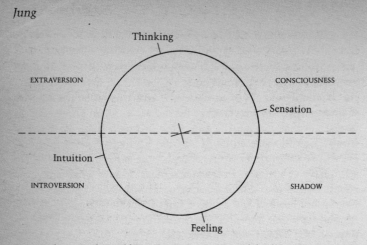

FIG. 2. The attitudes and functions in an extraverted thinking-sensation type

The other two functions remain relatively unconscious and associated with the shadow. The more unconscious of these is known as the *inferior* function. Thus, it is unusual to find thinking *and* feeling, sensation *and* intuition, developed in the same person. As a result, the rational functions, thinking and feeling, can be conceived as a pair of opposites, as can the irrational functions, sensation and intuition. An extraverted thinking-sensation type, therefore, would have an introverted feeling-intuitive shadow, and vice versa. This can be represented diagrammatically (Fig. 2).

In *Psychological Types* Jung gives a full and entertaining account of each of the eight theoretical types. Here it is possible to give no more than a thumbnail sketch of each type, together with a brief mention of its shadow opposite (which can be evident to those who have dealings with the person concerned).

Extraverted sensation types

People of this type are primarily concerned with objective reality, with how things really *are*. Essentially down-to-earth and practical, they love details, and have little time for abstractions, values, or meanings. Their constant aim, says Jung, is 'to have sensations and if possible to enjoy them' (*CW* VI, para. 605). They actively seek thrills in dangerous sports and tend to be *bons viveurs* who live in the moment and, like Epimetheus, take little account of the future. As a result they can be excellent company. Their motto is: 'Eat, drink and be merry, for tomorrow we die.' However, they can seem superficial and 'soulless'. If they come to the notice of psychiatrists, it is usually on account of addiction, fetishism, or obsessive-compulsive neurosis.

Shadow: their inferior function is intuition, which, being introverted, is triggered by inner events and not related to outer happenings. When activated, it tends to give rise to negative hunches which are generally off-beam. As a result, people of this type may suddenly become paranoid or hostile for little apparent reason. Their crude, undifferentiated intuition can also carry them off, much to everyone else's surprise, into some esoteric cult such as anthroposophy, or some form of archaic mysticism.

Examples: engineers, business people, builders, racing drivers, jockeys, hang-gliders, mountaineers; Mr Gradgrind in Dickens's *Hard Times*, whose obsessive interest is in 'facts'.

Introverted sensation types

'Whereas the extraverted sensation type is guided by the intensity of objective influences,' says Jung, 'the introverted type is guided by the intensity of the subjective sensation excited by the objective stimulus' (*CW* VI, para. 650). Emma Jung, who considered herself to be of this type, described herself as being like a highly sensitized photographic plate. Every detail of a situation is noticed and can be recalled at will. Such people have vivid memories for sights, colours, passages in books, sounds, conversations, smells, tastes, tactile sensations, and so on.

Shadow: their inferior function is extraverted intuition, which, when activated, is triggered by outer events. Such intuition tends to be essentially negative, in that when introverted sensation types use what little intuition they have they usually pick up what is wrong in a situation: they are forever smelling rats and detecting flies in ointment. Often they are wrong in these hunches, but occasionally they score a bull's eye. 'Whereas extraverted intuition . . . [normally has] a "good nose" for objectively real possibilities, this archaicized intuition has an amazing flair for all the dangerous possibilities lurking in the background' (*CW* VI, para. 654). This can give rise to dark prophetic fantasies about what might happen in the outer world. When people of this type break down they tend to become paranoid.

Examples: the detailed descriptions of people and places in Thomas Mann's novels suggest that he belonged to this type; leading French impressionist painters, who reproduced their vivid inner impressions of reality, probably also tended to be introverted sensation types.

Extraverted thinking types

People of this type base their activities on intellectual considerations guided by external criteria. They are good at solving problems, reorganizing businesses, clarifying issues, and sorting the grain from the chaff. Almost invariably they concern themselves with outer conditions and not with theories or ideas. They love practical rules of thumb which they seek to apply to all situations in which they involve themselves. Because they subordinate feeling to thinking they can seem cold and aloof.

Shadow: introverted feeling. This gives rise to feelings and value-judgements which are crude, inappropriate, and poorly expressed. Extraverted thinkers tend to take their personal relationships for granted and to be unaware of the feelings of people around them. Their archaic feeling function can sometimes lead them into sudden political or religious conversions or equally sudden changes in personal loyalties.

Examples: lawyers, administrative civil servants, management consultants, practical scientists, and technicians; Voltaire, a brilliant thinker and atheist, who was a scourge of the Church throughout his life, was suddenly converted to Catholicism on his death-bed, and demanded extreme unction.

Introverted thinking types

The activities of this type are also based on intellectual considerations but they are guided by internal criteria. They tend to show little interest in events proceeding in the outer world, and are essentially concerned with theories and ideas. When one reads Jung's account of this type, one realizes that he is describing himself: 'What seems to it of paramount importance is the development and presentation of the subjective idea, of the initial symbolic image hovering darkly behind the mind's eye' (*CW* VI, para. 628). In fact, Jung's theory of psychological types is a good example of introverted thinking in action: it is a carefully thought-out system, devised in neat opposites and balances, then imposed, like all typologies, on the psychological data. Preferring to be left alone with their thoughts, people of this type often prefer solitude to company, and, such is their intellectual self-sufficiency, they are little concerned whether their ideas find general acceptance or not.

Shadow: extraverted feeling. This can become active in relation to external objects, but introverted thinkers have great difficulty in recognizing their feelings and in sharing them with others. Since feeling is primitive and largely unconscious it can express itself in quixotic and unpredictable ways: powerful affects can suddenly erupt when people or events do not behave in a way that the introverted thinker believes they 'ought' to behave; attachments can be formed to unsuitable partners—like the professor in *The Blue Angel* who becomes passionately committed to a prostitute—with disastrous consequences.

Examples: philosophers, 'intellectuals', mathematicians, 'pure' scientists; Bertrand Russell.

Extraverted feeling types

The feelings, values, and judgements of this type tend to be conventional and in harmony with those of the company they habitually frequent. As a result, they are affable and easy to get on with. They hate their own company and find introspection morbid and depressing. Popular with friends and work-mates, they can always be relied upon to rally round in times of need. If you are forced to take to your bed with a slipped disc or the flu, the friend who pops in to feed the cat and do the shopping may well be an extraverted feeling type.

Jung

Shadow: introverted thinking. Jung: 'the unconscious of this type contains first and foremost a peculiar kind of thinking, a thinking that is infantile, archaic, negative' (*CW* VI, para. 600). Such thinking is narrow, coarse, and cynical. It can find specious application in providing justification for the feeling state of the moment, a tactic which greatly irritates extraverted thinkers. If extraverted feeling types should take up an intellectual system they tend to become fanatical about it because they are unable to think it through. When these types break down they tend to develop either hysteria or mania.

Examples: actors, TV 'personalities', public relations experts; Goethe's Wagner (in *Faust*); Noel Coward, Oscar Wilde, Lady Ottoline Morrell, Mae West, Sir Thomas Beecham, Sarah Bernhardt.

Introverted feeling types

People of this type have a highly differentiated set of values which they tend to keep to themselves. They may have a covert influence on those around them, however, by virtue of the standards they embody in their way of life. They can provide a group with its ethical backbone, not by preaching or lecturing, but just by being there. Jung: 'They are mostly silent, inaccessible, hard to understand . . . harmonious, inconspicuous, giving an impression of pleasing repose . . . with no desire to affect others, to impress, influence, or change them in any way . . . there is little effort to respond to the real emotions of the other person . . . This type observes a benevolent though critical neutrality, coupled with a faint sense of superiority . . .' (*CW* VI, para. 640). With this type it is true that 'still waters run deep'.

Shadow: extraverted thinking. As with extraverted feeling types, this thinking is concrete and primitive, but being extraverted it tends to be slavishly tied to objective facts, and when people of this type do attempt to use their thinking function, they tend to get lost in detail, not being able to see the wood for the trees. Breakdown usually leads to depression.

74

Examples: Rainer Maria Rilke, who once wrote to a lady: 'I love you, but it's none of your business!' The Mona Lisa gives the impression of belonging to this type.

Extraverted intuitive types

People of this type habitually use their intuition to deal with outer reality. In contrast to sensation types, intuitives are not interested in things 'as they really are' but in what might be done with them. Jung: 'intuition is not mere perception, or vision, but an active, creative process that puts into the object just as much as it takes out' (*CW* VI, para. 610). Extraverted intuitives are quick to see the possibilities inherent in a given situation and are good at predicting future developments. But unless they have thinking as their auxiliary function, they are not good at staying with the projects they initiate and seeing them through to a satisfactory conclusion. Their gift is essentially innovative and they are bored with routine. They will take up new friends, hobbies, or ideas because of their interesting possibilities, and then just as quickly drop them when other possibilities come into view.

Shadow: introverted sensation. Jung: '[the intuitive] does have sensations, of course, but he is not guided by them as such; he uses them merely as starting points for his perceptions' (*CW* VI, para. 611). However, he is often completely unconscious of his sensations and, as a consequence, is prone not to notice when he is tired, cold, or hungry. When his introverted sensation does become active, it can cause him to misinterpret messages arriving from his own sense organs, with the result that he may become hypochondriacal, or indulge in fads about diet and exercise.

Examples: journalists, stockbrokers, entrepreneurs, dealers in 'futures', currency speculators, creative artists and fashion designers who anticipate the *nouvelle vague* before it breaks.

Introverted intuitive types

'[Introverted intuition] does not concern itself with external possibilities but with what the external object has released within' (*CW*

Jung

VI, para. 656). People of this type are inclined to make use of the mechanism of *reification* (i.e. they treat ideas, images, or insights as if they were real objects). 'For intuition, therefore, unconscious images acquire the dignity of things' (*CW* VI, para. 657). Like Jung himself, who was primarily an introverted intuitive type (with thinking as his auxiliary function), they have difficulty in communicating their ideas simply and in an organized way, for they pursue image after image, idea after idea, 'chasing after every possibility in the womb of the unconscious', as Jung says, while usually overlooking what personal implications these possibilities may have. 'Had this type not existed, there would have been no prophets in Israel' (*GW* VI, para. 658). They may have brilliant insights, which, if they can be bothered or sufficiently organized to communicate them, others proceed to build on.

Shadow: extraverted sensation. Because this is mostly unconscious, they are constantly in danger of losing touch with outer reality, and if they break down they become schizophrenic. Many have schizoid personalities, as did Jung himself as a boy. Vague about practical details and poorly oriented in space and time, they tend to forget appointments, are seldom punctual, and easily get lost in strange places. Their poor relationship to reality, combined with the depth of their insights, causes some to experience themselves as belonging to the 'misunderstood genius' category. Their attitude to sexuality can be crude and inappropriate, and they tend to make poor lovers since they are unaware of what is happening in their own or their partner's body.

Examples: Seers, prophets, poets, psychologists (not experimental or academic ones), artists, shamans, mystics, and cranks; Nietzsche (especially in *Thus Spake Zarathustra*); Swedenborg.

The reader should be warned that the above descriptions are necessarily over-simplified and do less than justice to the detailed exegesis offered by Jung. Those wishing to study the typology in detail are referred to chapter X in volume VI of the *Collected Works*.

Origins

The search for typical psychological characteristics was by no means confined to Jung. Looking for common denominators is the way that the thinking function invariably proceeds when confronted with complex data, and many other typologies have been devised from classical times up to the present. Interestingly, the categories into which these typologies are divided are commonly four in number. It is as if the mind has a natural propensity to orientate itself through a tetrad of paired oppositions. That indispensable instrument of orientation, the magnetic compass, is a case in point. In the fifth century BC, the Greek philosopher Empedocles held that a tetrad of elements—earth and air, fire and water—was ruled by a great archetypal pair of opposites, Love and Strife. At about the same time, four primary qualities were defined—hot and cold, wet and dry—which also made up a tetrad of opposites, as did the four blood types of Aristotle and the four humours of Hippocrates. These ancient classificatory systems found modern expression in Rorschach's *Theory of Types* (1921) and Kretschmer's *Physique and Character* (1921) about the same time as Jung published *Psychological Types*.

Jung's motive in devising his typology was derived only in part from his wish to explain why he and Adler had quarrelled with Freud; it was also, I believe, a further attempt to compensate for his sense of personal oddity and isolation. Just as he had to discover what he shared in common with the rest of humanity, so he had also to explain how he was different.

Accordingly, he embarked on an extensive investigation of some of the great quarrels of history (e.g. those between St Augustine and Pelagius, Tertullian and Origen, Luther and Zwingli) and some of the major categorical distinctions made by philosophers and poets in the past (e.g. Nietzsche's contrast between the Apollonian and Dionysian, Spitteler's between Prometheus and Epimetheus, and Goethe's between the principles of diastole and systole). In all instances, he concluded, the distinctions represented a fundamental difference between extraverted and introverted attitudes.

In addition, he based his presentation on empirically gained insights derived from the observation of many different individuals. He was touchy on this point, for when his typology was attacked by academic psychologists they drew a tart riposte in his preface to the seventh edition of *Psychological Types*: 'my typology is the result of many years of practical experience, and such experience is, of course, not available to the academic psychologist . . .'!

One important source of the two attitude types is, however, conspicuously absent from Jung's extensive review of the literature, and that is the French psychologist Alfred Binet's distinction (made in his *L'Étude experimentale de l'intelligence*, 1903) between two types of intellectual attitude, which he termed 'introspection' and 'externospection'. Introspection he defined as 'the knowledge we have of our inner world, our thoughts, our feelings'; while externospection is 'the orientation of our knowledge toward the exterior world as opposed to the knowledge of ourselves' (Ellenberger, *The Discovery of the Unconscious*, 702–3). Since Binet's distinction, to say nothing of his terminology, is so close to Jung's it is strange that no mention is made of it in *Psychological Types*. The most charitable interpretation of his silence is that, in developing his ideas about the introverted and extraverted attitude types, Jung was experiencing a *cryptomnesia* (lit. hidden memory)—that although he had lost all conscious recollection of Binet's work, it had none the less borne fruit in his personal unconscious.

Use of the typology

Jung's typology is open to the same objection as all other typologies, namely, that it seeks to constrain the apparently infinite variety of human psychological traits within narrow, arbitrarily imposed categories. However, it must be said in his defence that Jung, the great individualist, was intensely aware of this problem, stating his conviction that 'every individual is an exception to the rule'. He goes on:

One can never give a description of a type, no matter how complete, that would apply to more than one individual, despite the fact that in some ways it aptly characterizes thousands of others. Conformity is one side of a man, uniqueness is the other. Classification does not explain the individual psyche. Nevertheless, an understanding of psychological types opens the way to a better understanding of human psychology in general.   (*CW* VI, para. 895)

'Pure' types do not exist. No one has just one function and one attitude and nothing else. We are all an amalgam. With some people it is easy to work out which function and which attitude habitually dominates, with others it is virtually impossible. This Jung freely admits: 'it is often very difficult to find out whether a person belongs to one type or the other, especially in regard to oneself.' With regard to the attitude types, he says: 'everyone possesses both mechanisms, extraversion as well as introversion, and only the relative predominance of one or the other determines the type. Hence, in order to throw the picture into the necessary relief, one would have to retouch it rather vigorously, and this would amount to a more or less pious fraud' (*CW* VI, para. 4).

The aspect of Jung's typology which has found widest acceptance is, in fact, his distinction between introverted and extraverted attitude types. Even Professor Hans Eysenck of London University, who has always been hostile to all forms of analysis, has confirmed the existence of an extraversion–introversion axis in the human personality, using the most carefully controlled quantitative techniques. Attempts to establish Jung's four functional types on an empirical basis have been less successful, however.

Jung argued that one's type was as much determined by genetic as by environmental factors, and it would indeed seem likely that both extraverted and introverted attitudes are biologically adaptive. Our predominant position on this planet is the direct result of our ability to adapt to changing environmental conditions on the one hand, and to reflect on ways of effectively meeting them on the other. In so complicated a species as *Homo sapiens* it is appropriate that some individuals should be genetically predisposed to specialize in an extraverted orientation and others to specialize in an introverted one.

Both extraverted and introverted attitudes are necessary for healthy development and all of us alternate in some degree between these two orientations. After all, even the most extraverted people fall every night into a profoundly introverted state when they go to sleep and begin to dream. In the dreaming state one is wholly withdrawn from the outer world and, for as long as it lasts, the dream represents the sum total of one's experience of reality.

In developing the theory of psychological types, Jung realized something extremely important that the academic psychologists tended to overlook, namely, that it is not possible for a psychologist to be entirely objective in collecting and interpreting his data. Unless the observer can know his own 'personal equation' and allow for it in his work, his observations must inevitably be vitiated by bias. Even in physics, it has been found that the scientist affects the phenomena he is observing; how much truer must this be in the study of human psychology and in the practice of analysis. Knowledge of one's type is useful, therefore, in that it enables one to correct in some measure the personal biases one brings to a situation.

On the whole, Jung's typology is best used in the way that one would use a compass: all typological possibilities are theoretically available to the Self, but it is useful to be able to establish those co-ordinates that one is using to chart one's course through life. Jung accepted that this course is never intractably fixed; it may at any time be subject to alteration. Viewed in this light, awareness of one's psychological type is not a constraint but a liberation, for it can open up new navigational possibilities in life, the existence of which one might otherwise never have discovered.

5   Dreams

The use of dreams is indispensable to classical Jungian analysis. Jung's theoretical approach to the dream was profoundly influenced by Freud's, first as a model for practical therapy, and later as a model to react against, to modify, and to extend. We must, therefore, take Freud's view of dreams as a starting-point.

Freud believed that during sleep forbidden wishes are liberated from their daytime inhibition and seek to gain admission to consciousness. However, the 'forbidden' nature of these wishes means that they are experienced by the ego as disturbing, and are therefore capable of waking one up. It is the function of dreams, in Freud's view, to prevent this from happening: they protect the ego by transforming the unacceptable wish into an acceptable set of images, thus enabling the dreamer to go on sleeping. 'All dreams are in a sense dreams of convenience,' wrote Freud in *The Interpretation of Dreams*: 'They serve the purpose of prolonging sleep instead of waking up. *Dreams are the GUARDIANS of sleep and not its disturbers*' (p. 330; Freud's italics).

The mental institution responsible for performing this protective function is the 'censor' or super-ego, which causes the forbidden wish (the *latent content* of the dream, as Freud called it) to be disguised and appear in a form which will neither disturb the ego nor wake the dreamer. The dream itself is thus the *manifest content* of the disguised wish. In order to disguise the latent content, the censor makes use of a number of techniques, such as *displacement*, *condensation*, *symbolization*, and *pictorialization*, and these defensive transformations account for the often bizarre or irrational nature of the manifest dream. Freud even goes so far as to make the circular argument that the bizarre nature of dreams is itself evidence for the existence and function of the censor in disguising the dream's true meaning.

The goal of Freudian dream interpretation is to undo the work of the censor. This is achieved by the technique of free association, whereby one starts with a dream image and allows one's thoughts to associate to it in complete freedom. As Freud put it: 'The restoration of the connections which the dream-work has destroyed is a task which has to be performed by the interpretative process' (ibid. 422). Thus: '*the interpretation of dreams is the royal road to a knowledge of the unconscious activities of the mind*' (ibid. 769; Freud's italics). In other words, the dream is a code to be decoded, a scrambled line to be unscrambled, so that its images can be reduced to their basic meanings.

Freud was satisfied that with these formulations he had solved the riddle that had intrigued mankind since antiquity, namely, how to unravel the meaning of dreams. He became so convinced of this when he was on holiday in Belle Vue Castle near Vienna in 1895 that he had the fantasy that one day a marble tablet would record that '*In this house on July 24th, 1895, the Secret of Dreams was revealed to Dr. Sigmund Freud*'.

Initially, Jung went along with Freud's approach, but he was quick to see its limitations, and his growing reservations were similar to those that he entertained about psychoanalysis as a whole. Freud believed that dreams fashioned their manifest content out of memory residues from two sources: from events of the previous day and from childhood. Jung accepted this, but, as we have seen, he went much further, maintaining that dreams draw on a third, much deeper source, belonging to the evolutionary history of our species, which he called the collective unconscious. Moreover, Freud believed that the forbidden wishes responsible for the production of dreams were predominantly sexual in origin. Jung, on the other hand, was convinced that dreams had their origins in much wider concerns, namely, the basic issues of human existence.

After the break with Freud and his encounter with the unconscious, Jung felt free to develop his own approach to dreams, though, unlike Freud, he was never dogmatic about it. On the contrary, he was capable of undue modesty: 'I have no theory about dreams,' he wrote, 'I do not know how dreams arise. And I am not at all sure that my way of handling dreams even deserves the name of a "method"' (*CW* XVI, para. 86). Having issued this disclaimer, however, he proceeded to reject the basic tenets of Freud's dream theory and replace them with suggestions of his own.

In fact, most of Freud's hypotheses have proved untenable in the light of dream research, while Jung's have stood up to the test of time. For example, the well-established observation that all mammals dream and that human infants devote much of their time to REM (rapid eye movement) dream sleep, both in the womb and post-natally, would seem to dispose of the idea that dreams are disguised expressions of repressed wishes or that their primary function is to preserve sleep. It is more likely that dreams are, as Jung maintained, natural products of the psyche, that they perform some homeostatic or self-regulatory function, and that they obey the biological imperative of adaptation in the interests of personal adjustment, growth, and survival.

Jung's theory of dreams can be summarized under four headings:

1. Dreams are natural, spontaneous events, which proceed independently of conscious will or intention;
2. Dreams are both purposive and compensatory, in that they serve to promote the balance and individuation of the personality;
3. The symbols of dreams are true symbols, not signs, and they possess a transcendent function;
4. The therapeutic power of dreams is better served by the techniques of *amplification* and *active imagination* than by interpretation based on 'free association'.

We shall consider each of these in turn.

Pure nature

Dreams are impartial, spontaneous products of the unconscious psyche, outside the control of the will. They are pure nature; they show us the unvarnished, natural truth, and are therefore fitted, as nothing else is, to give us back an attitude that accords with our basic human nature when our consciousness has strayed too far from its foundations and run into an impasse. (*CW* X, para. 317)

'They do not deceive, they do not lie, they do not distort or disguise . . . They are invariably seeking to express something that the ego does not know and does not understand' (*CW* XVII, para. 189). The dream is 'a spontaneous self-portrayal in symbolic form, of the actual situation in the unconscious' (*CW* VIII, para. 505).

Certainly, it is not a façade designed to conceal what lies behind it:

Cornell West

the so-called façade of most houses is by no means a fake or a deceptive distortion; on the contrary, it follows the plan of the building and often betrays the interior arrangement. The 'manifest' dream-picture is the dream itself and contains the whole meaning of the dream. When I find sugar in the urine it is sugar and not just a façade for albumen. What Freud calls 'the dream façade' is the dream's obscurity, and this is really only a projection of our own lack of understanding. We say that the dream has a false front only because we fail to see into it. (*CW* XVI, para. 319)

Jung was fond of quoting the Talmud to the effect that 'The dream is its own interpretation'. Why then do dreams need to be interpreted? Not because they are *disguises* but because their meanings are formulated in a pictorial 'language' that is rendered comprehensible to the ego only when put into words.

'The whole dream-work is essentially subjective, and a dream is a theatre in which the dreamer is himself the scene, the player, the prompter, the producer, the author, the public, and the critic' (*CW* VIII, para. 509).

The view that dreams are merely the imaginary fulfilments of repressed wishes is hopelessly out of date. There are, it is true, dreams which manifestly represent wishes or fears, but what about all the other things? Dreams may contain ineluctable truths, philosophical pronouncements, illusions, wild fantasies, memories, plans, anticipations, irrational experiences, even telepathic visions, and heaven knows what besides. (*CW* XVI, para. 317)

Compensatory function

Jung's proposition that dreams perform a compensatory function in balancing the one-sided attitudes of ego-consciousness is consistent with his concept of psychic homeostasis. The passage, quoted above on pp. 54–5, in which Jung asserts that 'the theory of compensation is a basic law of psychic behaviour' continues: 'Too little on one side results in too much on the other. Similarly, the relation between conscious and unconscious is compensatory. This is one of the best-proven rules of dream interpretation. When we set out to interpret a dream, it is always helpful to ask: What conscious attitude does it compensate?' (*CW* XVI, para. 330).

Thus dreams 'add something important to our conscious knowledge', and 'a dream which fails to do so has not been properly interpreted' (*CW* XVI, para. 318). Dreams 'always stress the other side in order to maintain the psychic equilibrium' (*CW* VII, para. 170).

In one sense, Jung's compensatory concept may be seen as an extension of Freud's theory of wish-fulfilment, for both conceive dreams as a means of making accessible to consciousness something previously unavailable and unconscious. But whereas Freud held the purpose of the dream to be one of deception so as to outwit the censor and enable the shadow to enter consciousness in disguise, Jung thought its purpose was to serve individuation by making valuable unconscious potential available to the whole personality. In contrast to Freud's causal or reductive approach, which traced dream contents back to their infantile instinctual origins, Jung advocated a constructive, teleological approach which sought to discover where the dream contents might be leading. For Jung, the prospective implications of a dream were more significant for personality development (and for a positive therapeutic outcome) than its possible origins in earlier personal experiences. To plough a symbol back into its past was to deprive the dreamer of its contribution to the present and the future, and to adopt an essentially reductive standpoint was to negate the creative, goal-seeking powers of the psychic system. 'No psychological fact can ever be explained in terms of causality alone; as a living phenomenon, it is always indissolubly bound up with the continuity of the vital process, so that it is not only something evolved but also continually evolving and creative' (*CW* VI, para. 717).

Accordingly, dreams serve the teleological imperative of the Self, which works unceasingly towards its own realization in life. (*Teleo* is a combination word derived from *teleos*, meaning perfect, complete, and *telos*, meaning end; *teleology*, therefore, is about attaining the goal of completeness.)

Symbolism

No area of disagreement between Jung and Freud reflected more clearly the temperamental differences between them than their respective attitude to symbols. To Freud, a symbol was a figurative representation of an unconscious idea, conflict, or wish. It was a substitute-formation which effectively disguised the true meaning of the idea it represented: a sword was a symbol of the penis, its sheath a symbol of the vagina, and pushing the sword into its sheath a symbol of sexual intercourse.

For his part, Jung did not consider the Freudian symbol to be a symbol at all; it was a *sign*, for it regularly referred to something already known or knowable and embodied a meaning that was fixed. Jung's understanding of symbols was quite different. To him symbols were living entities striving to express something previously unknown; they were intuitive ideas that, at the moment of their creation, could not be formulated in any better way (*CW* XV, para. 105). Thus, symbols 'mean more than they say' and remain 'a perpetual challenge to our thoughts and feelings' (*CW* XV, para. 119).

These different approaches to symbolism are a further expression of Freud's reductive orientation on the one hand and Jung's teleological orientation to the psyche and its functions on the other. To Jung, symbols were natural growth factors which made possible the development of the personality, the resolution of conflict, and the transcendence of polar oppositions. For this reason, he held that symbols possessed a *transcendent function*, facilitating all transitions from one psychological state to another. Symbols are, therefore, indispensable to healing and to the individuation of the Self. Human beings owe their pre-eminent status in the world to the fact that they are symbol-making animals.

Consideration of the transcendent function brings us to the heart of Jung's love of paradox and his celebration of the generative power of *opposites*. 'The opposites are the ineradicable and indispensable preconditions of all psychic life,' he wrote (*CW* XIV, para. 206). All opposites are intrinsically irreconcilable: but conflict between any pair of opposites generates tension which motivates the psyche to seek a third possibility that transcends them both. If one can learn to bear the tension that oppositions invariably bring, then the problem is raised to a higher plane: good is reconciled with evil, love with hate, doubt with certainty, and a new synthesis will follow between conscious and unconscious, persona and shadow, ego and Self. Such reconciliations are attained neither rationally nor intellectually, but symbolically, through *the transcendent function of symbols*.

Creative work with symbols is, therefore, the key to successful personal development and therapeutic practice.

Interpretation

In working on a dream the starting-point for Jung was not interpretation but 'amplification'—that is, to enter into the atmosphere of the dream, to establish its mood as well as the detail of its images and symbols, in such a way as to *amplify the experience of the dream itself*. Then its impact on consciousness is enhanced.

Because every symbol encompasses more than can be said about it, it must not be 'reduced' to its origins, but its implications examined in an archetypal light. Instead of breaking the dream down into a series of intellectual formulations, one should *circumambulate* its symbols (lit. walk round about them) allowing them to reveal their different facets to consciousness. Personal associations need to be taken into account, but a full appreciation of the dream's intention cannot stop there if one is to receive all that it has to offer.

Though most remembered dreams are little more than fragments or a few brief episodes, many have a story to tell and take the form of a private drama. In these a definite structure can be perceived, which Jung divided into four stages: (1) the *exposition*, which sets the place and often the time of the action, as well as the dramatis personae involved; (2) the *development* of the plot, in which the situation becomes complicated and 'a definite tension develops because one does not know what will happen'; (3) the *culmination* or *peripeteia*, when 'something decisive happens or something changes completely'; and (4) the *lysis*, the conclusion, the solution, or result of the dream-work (*CW* VIII, paras. 361–4).

An example will help to make these points clear.

[I was] in a mountainous region on the Swiss-Austrian border. It was toward evening, and I saw an elderly man in the uniform of an Imperial Austrian customs official [stage 1: the *exposition*]. He walked past, somewhat stooped, without paying any attention to me. His expression was peevish, rather than melancholic and vexed [stage 2: the *development*]. There were other persons present, and someone informed me that the old man was not really there, but was the ghost of a customs official who had died years ago

[stage 3: the *peripeteia*]. 'He is one of those who still couldn't die properly'
[stage 4: the *lysis*].   (*MDR* 158)

This is not the end of the dream, however, as the dreamer is
transported to another place and a similar narrative structure is
repeated: he now finds himself in a city.

The city was Basel, and yet it was also an Italian city, something like
Bergamo. It was summertime; the blazing sun stood at the zenith, and
everything was bathed in an intense light [*Exposition*]. A crowd came
streaming toward me, and I knew that the shops were closing and people
were on their way home to dinner [*Development*]. In the midst of this
stream of people walked a knight in full armour. He mounted the steps
toward me. He wore a helmet of the kind that is called a basinet, with eye
slits, and chain armour. Over this was a white tunic into which was woven,
front and back, a large red cross [*Peripeteia*]. . . . I asked myself what this
apparition meant, and then it was as if someone answered me—but there
was no one there to speak: 'Yes, this is a regular apparition. The knight
always passes by here between twelve and one o'clock, and has been doing
so for a very long time (for centuries, I gathered) and everyone knows about
it' [*Lysis*].   (*MDR* 160)

The first thing that strikes one about the dream as a whole is the
powerfully arresting quality of its mood and imagery, as well as the
stark contrast apparent between the sad, ghostly customs official
and the extraordinary, surreal presence of the medieval knight.
That the dream opens on the Swiss-Austrian border must carry
some significance, as must the dress, appearance, and manner of
the customs official. Why should he not be there and why can he
not die properly? Why is the knight, who should have died so long
age, seen striding through the streets of a modern city? While the
former is old and worn out, a has-been, the latter is imbued with
the vibrant intensity of an archetypal image—the knight in shining
armour. What does this mean?

In Jungian therapy, it is customary to approach a dream in three
stages. The first attempts to establish the context of the dream in
the life of the dreamer, so as to understand something of its purely
personal significance. Next, the cultural context of the dream has
to be defined, since it is invariably related to the milieu and time
in which is was dreamt. Finally, the archetypal content is explored
so as to set the dream in the context of human life as a whole, since

at the most profound level dreams link us with the age-old experience of our species.

In practice it is seldom possible to keep these stages separate because, inevitably, the personal, cultural, and archetypal components of experience, as well as interpretations of their meaning, constantly interact. However, in the interests of clarity, we will consider the elements of this dream under three headings, while tolerating the unavoidable overlap between them.

Personal context

Much of the personal context has already been revealed (pp. 12–16 above): the dream was dreamt by Jung shortly before he broke off his friendship with Freud. To be more precise, it occurred while Jung was working on his book *Transformations and Symbols of the Libido* (*CW* V, *Symbols of Transformation*), in which he expressed ideas which he feared would prove unacceptable to Freud. The associations which Jung reports to the dream are brief and to the point, for he did not advocate uninhibited use of free association as did Freud. To Jung, association only facilitated dream interpretation as long as it was confined to the images in the dream. Freudian free association, in Jung's view, carried the dreamer away from the dream and served only to lead him back, time and again, to his childhood complexes, and this defeated the object of the exercise.

With the word *customs* Jung says he at once associated the word 'censorship', and in association with *border* he thought of the border between consciousness and the unconscious on the one hand, and between his views and Freud's on the other.

Of the knight Jung says:

One can easily imagine how I felt: suddenly to see in a modern city, during the noonday rush hour, a crusader coming toward me. What struck me as particularly odd was that none of the many persons walking about seemed to notice him. . . . it was as though he were completely invisible to everyone but me. . . . even in the dream, I knew that the knight belonged to the twelfth century. That was the period when alchemy was beginning and also the quest for the Holy Grail. The stories of the Grail had been of the greatest importance to me ever since I read them, at the age of fifteen, for the first time. I had an inkling that a great secret still lay hidden behind those stories. Therefore it seemed quite natural to me that the dream should conjure up the world of the Knights of the Grail and their quest—for that was, in the deepest sense, my own world, which had scarcely anything to do with Freud's. My whole being was seeking for something still unknown which might confer meaning on the banality of life. (*MDR* 158–61)

Cultural context

A frontier is an agreed line of demarcation separating two states: in terms of dream logic, it makes little difference whether these be nation states or states of mind. What cannot be overlooked is that Freud's state is Austria and Jung's Switzerland; and Freud, in some official 'imperial' role, is patrolling the border between them. At a frontier, one's personal belongings are subject to scrutiny, one's suitcases opened and searched for contraband, and one's passport examined to ensure that one's credentials are in order, and all this is done by a customs officer. Could this be a reference to the subject-matter of psychoanalysis (the borderline between consciousness and the unconscious) and to Freud as the master analyst, peevish, vexed, and sad because he suspects the dreamer is harbouring ideas that are both subversive and objectionable? In reflecting on the dream, Jung certainly made this connection. But why, he asked himself, should he dream of Freud as the ghost of a customs inspector? 'Could that be the death-wish which Freud had insinuated I had felt toward him?' He thought not, for he had no reason for wishing Freud dead. Rather he saw the dream as compensating and correcting his conscious attitude to Freud, which he now perceived as unduly deferential. The dream was recommending a more critical, more robust manner in his dealings with Freud.

The confusion between Basel and Italy in the second part of the dream is probably a reference to the achievement of Jung's fellow Baseler, Jakob Burckhardt, who linked the civilization of their home town with that of the Renaissance in Italy. This Italy is the world of anima and love, of Dante and Beatrice, Petrarch and Laura, of art and the rebirth of the human spirit. That the sun is at its zenith as the people stream home from the shops evokes the enantiodromia of mid-life, as Jung described it (p. 61 above): 'At the stroke of noon the descent begins. And the descent means the reversal of all the ideals and values that were cherished in the morning.' The first half of life is the life of 'getting and spending', but now the shops are shut and this phase is over. What promise does the future bring? The answer appears in the extraordinary figure of the knight, dressed in armour; not a man of the future, but an archetypal figure from the past, the Christian gentleman, the chivalrous warrior. He belongs to the twelfth century, which Jung associates with the beginnings of alchemy and the emergence of the legend of the Holy Grail.

Archetypal context

The archetypal images of greatest significance in this dream are the vessel (the Grail), the knight/warrior, and the cross. These in turn, and by association, bring up the archetypal themes of the old and dying king, the wounded healer, and the shaman/magician.

According to legend, the Grail was the vessel used by Jesus at the Last Supper and later by Joseph of Arimathea to collect and preserve the Saviour's blood after the Crucifixion. It is thus the most precious object in Christendom. The theme of the miraculous vessel is much older than Christianity, however. As Freud would have been the first to agree, the Grail or vessel is a feminine symbol, a womb in which a miraculous, life-giving transformation occurs. The vessel or *vas* was central to the alchemical tradition which began in ancient China and reached Northern Europe, as Jung comments, in the twelfth century. The Gnostics, with whom Jung felt a close affinity, believed that one of the original gods had made a gift to humanity of a *krater*, a mixing vessel, in which those who sought spiritual transformation were immersed. This Gnostic tradition seems to have entered European alchemy through the influence of Zosimos of Panopolis, one of the earliest and most influential alchemists, whose visions were later to be of great interest to Jung. The medieval mystics adopted the vessel as a symbol of the soul, which exists to be filled and replenished endlessly by Divine Grace.

The association of the Grail legend with England and King Arthur's Knights of the Round Table came through the figure of Merlin, the great magician, shaman, and bard of Celtic mythology. Merlin was born of an illicit union between the devil and an innocent virgin and thus emerged as a counterbalance to the figure of Christ. Early in his career, Merlin presides over a dragon fight which results in the deposition of the old usurper King Vertigier and his replacement by King Uter, to whom Merlin confides the secret of the Grail, instructing Uter to set up a Third Table. The

First Table was that of the Last Supper; the Second was the Table on which Joseph of Arimathea had kept the Grail, and it was *square*; the Third Table, which King Uter will provide, must be *round*. This rounding of the square is the very essence of the *mandala* configuration and symbolizes the achievement of wholeness, the complete realization of the Self. The quest for the Holy Grail is the individuation quest undertaken *sub specie aeternitatis*.

The Grail legend fascinated Jung all his life. As a boy he read Malory and Froissart and of all music he loved Wagner's *Parsifal* the most. He would have devoted as much time to the Grail as to alchemy had not his wife expressed a strong wish to do the work herself. As far as the dream is concerned, the most interesting aspect of the legend, apart from the vessel itself, is the theme of the 'old sick king', Amfortas. Like Chiron in Greek mythology, Amfortas suffers from a wound which will not heal; and the fascinating aspect of this wound is its situation: it is in the thigh or genital region. Amfortas's wound is a sexual wound, his problem a sexual problem. He wishes to relinquish his kingly authority and pass it on to Parsifal, much as Freud wished to hand his over to Jung, but he cannot do so until Parsifal questions him about the Grail.

Jung himself did not make this connection between Amfortas and Freud, but he made it with his own father, who was the psychological precursor of Freud in his life: 'My memory of my father is of a sufferer stricken with an Amfortas wound, a "fisher king" whose wound would not heal—that Christian suffering for which the alchemists sought the panacea. I, as a "dumb" Parsifal was the witness of this sickness during the years of my boyhood, and, like Parsifal, speech failed me. I had only inklings' (*MDR* 205).

Freud was no less a 'fisher king', and in his presence Jung was no less incapable of speech than Parsifal, never putting to Freud the question about his service to the god of sex. That is why their relationship lasted as long as it did.

Under the impress of Freud's personality I had, as far as possible, cast aside my own judgements and repressed my criticisms. That was the prerequisite for collaborating with him. I had told myself, 'Freud is far wiser and more experienced than you. For the present you must simply listen to what he says and learn from him.' And then, to my own surprise, I found myself dreaming of him as a peevish official of the Imperial Austrian monarchy, as a defunct and still walking ghost of a customs inspector! (*MDR* 159)

The symbolism of the cross needs little amplification: it indicates the cardinal points of the mandala and is the Christian symbol of wholeness, representing the reconciliation of opposites through suffering, the memorial of Christ's individuation and at-one-ment with God. The cross stands for the path of submission to one's personal destiny as a human being, for the alchemist no less than the Christian.

Submission to the fundamental contrariety of human nature amounts to an acceptance of the fact that the psyche is at cross purposes with itself. Alchemy teaches that the tension is four-fold, forming a cross which stands for the four warring elements. The quaternity is the minimal aspect under which such a state of total opposition can be regarded. The 'cross' as a form of suffering expresses psychic reality, and carrying the cross is therefore an apt symbol for the wholeness and the passion which the alchemist saw in his work. (*CW* XVI, para. 523)

The solitary crusader is the Christian soldier, marching as to war. He has a goal, a destiny which he has no choice but to fulfil. It is an image of what Jung was to become, not as a Christian but as a man. 'If a man knows more than others, he becomes lonely,' he wrote at the end of his life.

There was a daimon in me . . . it overpowered me . . . I could never stop at anything once attained. I had to hasten on, to catch up with my vision. Since my contemporaries could not perceive my vision, they saw only a fool rushing ahead . . . I was able to become intensely interested in people; but as soon as I had seen through them, the magic was gone. In this way I made many enemies. A creative person has little power over his own life. He is not free. He is captive and drawn by his daimon . . . This lack of freedom has been a great sorrow to me. Often I felt as if I were on a battlefield, saying, 'Now you have fallen, my good comrade, but I must go on.' (*MDR* 328–9)

Enough has been said for the reader to appreciate that the analysis of a dream in a manner advocated by Jung is a discursive process requiring considerable erudition as well as a gift for symbolic understanding. Much more is involved than a mere interpretation of the basic message, which in this case might be stated simply as, 'Get rid of Freud and go your own way'.

Before becoming a medical student, Jung had toyed with the idea of studying archaeology, and it was a subject which never lost its fascination for him. As he often said, he approached a dream as if it were an undeciphered text and he used all his archaeological instincts in the endeavour. Only when one has excavated the personal, cultural, and archetypal foundations of the dream is one in a position to appreciate its implications. Then, as one strolls round the site of one's excavations the dream's architecture stands revealed, together with a sense of what the architect was seeking to achieve, and where all his creative energy could lead. It is a delicate process of sifting, cataloguing, and comparing, requiring much imaginative flair: the dream must never be excavated to destruction, but its atmosphere savoured and its message left intact.

As Jung discovered, themes which are of great importance in somebody's life tend to repeat, as can be verified by studying a series of dreams from the same dreamer. Jung himself returned to the theme of the Grail in a dream he had in India in 1938 and this, like his dream of the crusader, linked him with his childhood fantasy of the castle on its rocky promontory. In the dream, he found himself, with a number of his Zürich friends and acquaintances, on an unknown island off the south coast of England. It was a long, narrow strip of land and on the rocky coast at its southern end was a medieval castle. 'Before us rose an imposing *beffroi*, through whose gate a wide stone staircase was visible. We could just manage to see that it terminated above in a columned hall. This hall was dimly illuminated by candlelight. I understood that this was the castle of the Grail, and that this evening there would be a "celebration of the Grail" here . . .' (*MDR* 262).

The world of the knight, the Grail, and of Merlin, was not Freud's world but *his* world—the world of the castle on the rock with its copper column and alchemical laboratory. The trouble with the modern world, like the origin of neurosis, was not so much sexual repression as 'loss of soul', a lack of perception of the sacred. Freud's contribution only served to compound the plight of our culture for he struggled to find the sacred in one basic instinct, sex. The knightly ideal, one of the noblest expressions of the European spirit, was being ignored. The knight's Holy Quest was degenerating into the 'waste land' of our post-Christian civilization.

This theme, too, recurred in another dream in which he found himself surrounded by sarcophagi dating from Merovingian times. Then he passed by dead figures from the eighth century and went on until he came to some twelfth-century tombs, where he stopped before the corpse of 'a crusader in chain mail who lay there with clasped hands. His figure seemed carved out of wood. For a long time I looked at him and thought he was really dead. But suddenly I saw that a finger of his left hand was beginning to stir gently' (*MDR* 167).

The knight is still alive in his unconscious, offering him a way forward out of the past, away from the moribund figure of Freud, the vexed customs officer. But it is a future and a past (red cross on the front and on the back of the crusader) that is marked by the Christian symbol for wholeness and redemption, the state of at-one-ment with God. He would have to go on like the knight, his progress ignored by the populace around him, supported only by the flickering of his own 'little light' and by the few congenial souls he was to collect at his own Round Table.

6 Therapy

It is not possible within the confines of one chapter to give an adequate account of the profound transformation that Jungian analysis at its best can bring, or give anything more than a cursory outline of the principles on which its practice is based. However, the task must be attempted since the school of analysis that is carried on in Jung's name is his chief legacy to our culture.

The innovations introduced by Jung have had an influence which extends far beyond his own school, and it is fair to say that this influence has been benevolent and humane. His initial formulations arose mainly out of his own 'creative illness', as we have seen, but they were also a reaction against the stereotype of the classical Freudian analyst, sitting silent and aloof behind the couch, occasionally emitting *ex cathedra* pronouncements and interpretations, while remaining totally uninvolved in the patient's anguish and sufferings. Instead, Jung offered the radical proposal that analysis is a *dialectical* procedure, a two-way exchange between two people, who are equally involved. Although this was a revolutionary idea when he first suggested it, it is a model which has influenced psychotherapists of most schools, though many seem not to realize that it originated with Jung.

Jung's contribution to the practice of psychotherapy can be considered for convenience under four headings: (1) his approach to mental illness, (2) his attitude to patients, (3) the principles and techniques he advocated in treatment, and (4) his views on the role of the therapist.

Illness

In formulating his approach to mental illness, Jung was reacting not only against the concepts of Freudian psychoanalysis but also against the ideas which prevailed, and to a large extent still prevail, in conventional psychiatry. The truth is that Jung's experience was wider and his mentality more far-sighted than was generally the case among practitioners of either of these disciplines. Freud had

96

tested and (to his own satisfaction) confirmed his hypotheses on the basis of his analyses of a small group of upper-middle-class Austrian patients, mostly women suffering from hysteria (a condition much in vogue at the end of the nineteenth century, but seldom diagnosed today). Jung's patients, on the other hand, came, at least initially, from all walks of life and exhibited practically every condition described in Krafft-Ebing's *Textbook of Psychiatry*. Moreover, Jung based his formulations not only on himself and his patients but on an extensive study of myths, comparative religion, and anthropology in a Herculean effort to establish universal truths which would be valid for all human beings, irrespective of their class, race, or creed. Above all, he did his best to remain undogmatic to the end. When his English colleague, E. A. Bennet, told Jung in 1951 that he was writing an article about him for the *British Medical Journal*, he said at once: 'Whatever you say, make it clear that I have no dogma, I'm still open and haven't got things fixed.'

The open-minded humanity of his approach to mental illness was evident from the beginning of his work at the Burghölzli as Bleuler's assistant. Unlike the great majority of psychiatrists at the time, Jung, as we have already noted (p. 12 above), actually listened to what his patients said to him, however deluded or hallucinated they might be. As he wrote much later:

In many cases in psychiatry, the patient who comes to us has a story that is not told, and which as a rule no one knows of. To my mind, therapy only really begins after the investigation of that wholly personal story. It is the patient's secret, the rock against which he is shattered. If I know his secret story, I have a key to the treatment. . . . In therapy the problem is always the whole person, never the symptom alone. We must ask questions which challenge the whole personality. (*MDR* 118)

By attending carefully to what his psychotic patients told him, he says,

I realized that paranoid ideas and hallucinations contain a germ of meaning. A personality, a life history, a pattern of hopes and desires lie behind the psychosis. The fault is ours if we do not understand them. It dawned upon me then for the first time that a general psychology of the personality lies concealed within psychosis, and that even here we come upon the old human conflicts. Although patients may appear dull and apathetic, or totally imbecilic, there is more going on in their mind, and more that is meaningful, than there seems to be. At bottom we discover nothing new and unknown in the mentally ill, rather we encounter the substratum of our own natures. (*MDR* 127)

This was even more true in the case of neurosis: 'The psychic processes of neurotics differ hardly at all from those of so-called normal persons—for what man today is quite sure that he is not neurotic?' (*CW* VIII, para. 667).

Although he learned all about making psychiatric diagnoses at the Burghölzli, he felt the procedure to be of limited usefulness: 'Clinical diagnoses *are* important, since they give the doctor a certain orientation. But they do not help the patient. The crucial thing is the story. For it alone shows the human background and the human suffering, and only at that point can the doctor's therapy begin to operate' (*MDR* 124).

The old pathological approach, which persists in general psychiatry to this day, describes mental illnesses as distinct 'entia', each presenting a specific and clearly defined clinical picture. Jung considered this to be rewarding up to a point, but it had the disadvantage of thrusting all the inessential features of the condition to the forefront, while covering up the one aspect that is essential, namely, 'the fact that this illness is always an intensely individual phenomenon' (*CW* XVII, para. 203).

In very general terms, he believed schizophrenia (psychosis) and hysteria (neurosis) to be extreme expressions of the two basic attitude types—extreme introversion resulting in a withdrawal of libido from outer reality leading into an entirely private world of fantasy and archetypal imagery, and extreme extraversion leading away from a sense of inner integrity to an exaggerated concern with one's influence in the world of social relationships. In other words, schizophrenics live in the unconscious while hysterics live in their persona.

Put in its widest conceptual context, therefore, mental health and mental illness are both functions of homeostatic balance or imbalance between the needs of the individual and the demands of the collective. When people become neurotic it is because divisions have opened up within them, conscious and unconscious processes no longer operate in homeostatic balance. This 'disalliance with the unconscious' is 'synonymous with loss of instinct and rootlessness'. But 'if we can successfully develop that function which I have called transcendent, the disharmony ceases and we can then enjoy the favourable side of the unconscious. The unconscious then gives us all the encouragement and help that a bountiful nature can shower upon a man' (*CW* XIV, para. 502).

It is true that Jung's emphasis is invariably on the intra-psychic life of the individual, but he does not ignore the importance of adaptation to the demands of society:

Thus, from the psychological (not the clinical) point of view, we can divide the psychoneuroses into two main groups: the one comprising collective people with underdeveloped individuality, the other individualists with atrophied collective adaptation. The therapeutic attitude differs accordingly, for it is abundantly clear that a neurotic individualist can only be cured by recognizing the collective man in himself—hence the need for collective adaptation.   (*CW* XVI, para. 5)

Jung's view that psychiatric symptoms are persistent exaggerations of natural psychophysiological responses was not only shared by Freud but has been reaffirmed by contemporary psychiatrists who use ethological concepts in their approach to mental illness. For example, Dr Brant Wenegrat of the Stanford University Medical Centre in California sees all psychopathological syndromes, whether psychotic, neurotic, or psychopathic, as statistically abnormal manifestations of *innate response strategies* (his term for archetypes) shared by all individuals whether they are mentally healthy or ill.

Jung carried this insight one very important stage further, arguing that *symptom formation is itself a product of the individuation process*, that illness is an autonomously creative act, a function of the psyche's imperative to grow and develop having to proceed in abnormal circumstances. Neurosis is thus a form of adaptation, albeit 'inferior adaptation', of a potentially healthy organism responding to the demands of life. 'Because of some obstacle—a constitutional weakness or defect, wrong education, bad experiences, an unsuitable attitude, etc.—one shrinks from the difficulties which life brings . . .' (*CW* XIII, para. 472). Individuation is distorted or goes awry because the individual experiences difficulty in achieving a mature adjustment because certain archetypal needs essential to the programme of development have not been met at the appropriate time in the past.

However, this does not mean that Jung agreed with Freud that the origins of a neurosis invariably lie in early childhood. On the contrary, neurosis is caused by a failure to contend with contemporary circumstances. It may occur at any stage of the life cycle as a response to outer events, such as going to a new school, losing a parent, starting a new job, being conscripted into the Army, getting married, bearing one's first child, etc. Earlier traumata may predispose the individual to exhibit neurotic symptoms, it is true, but such traumata are not the *cause* of the neurosis. Neurosis is, therefore, in Jung's view, essentially an escape from a challenging life event which the individual feels unequipped to meet. Consequently, he taught his students, when confronted with a new patient, to ask themselves: 'What task is the patient trying to avoid?'

Not infrequently the patient's difficulty stops short of an incapacitating breakdown, but life is experienced as essentially unfulfilling and pointless.

I have frequently seen people become neurotic when they content themselves with inadequate or wrong answers to the questions of life. They seek position, marriage, reputation, outward success or money, and remain unhappy and neurotic even when they have attained what they were seeking. Such people are usually confined within too narrow a spiritual horizon. Their life has not sufficient content, sufficient meaning. If they are enabled to develop into more spacious personalities, the neurosis generally disappears. For that reason the idea of development was always of the highest importance to me.

Jung's understanding of symptom formation as a creative act is of the highest value for the development of therapeutic optimism in both patient and therapist, for instead of regarding the symptoms as representing a form of futile suffering, they can be seen as the growing pains of a soul struggling to escape fear and find fulfilment, as providing an invaluable opportunity to become conscious and to grow. Neurosis, he said, in the nearest he came to a definitive definition, is the suffering of a soul that has not found its meaning.

The patient

Many patients who consulted Jung have testified to the cordiality, warmth, and courtesy with which they were received. His sense of humour, always in evidence, made it impossible for him to seem pompous or self-important, and he never attempted to disguise his own fallibility as a human being. For example, he greeted one new and deeply worried patient with a reassuring grin, saying, 'So you're in the soup, too!' He believed in treating people as human beings rather than as 'patients' and taught that every appointment was a social occasion as well as a clinical interview. For that reason he never used a couch or any obvious techniques or tricks of the trade, treating everybody as essentially normal and healthy, while accepting, incidentally, that they might have a problem. 'If the person has a neurosis,' he said, 'that is something extra, but people should be regarded as normal and met socially' (Bennet, *Meetings with Jung*, 32).

What struck most of his patients was the extent to which he was *in* the analytic situation, completely *there*: not aloof and out of sight, not a screen for projections, not a transference manipulator, or a clinical manager, but there as a *real* person, wholly involved in the work, respecting the patient as an equal, not as a sick inferior. His keenness to abdicate all idea of personal superiority or of knowing all the answers, went along with a willingness to acknowledge his own vulnerability in the belief that 'only the wounded physician heals'. 'It's very important *not* to know all the answers,' he said. 'Often we *don't* know, and if we did it would be no good, for it is greater value to the patient when he discovers the answers himself' (ibid. 32).

My own analyst, Irene Champernowne, who was herself analysed by Jung, told me that he gave you the feeling that he was there not just because he was your analyst, but because, through you, he was pursuing his own research, that he too was learning from the process. This gave a sense of heightened importance to the proceedings. Jung himself acknowledged this in his autobiography: 'My patients brought me so close to the reality of human life that I could not help learning essential things from them. Encounters with people of so many different kinds and on so many different psychological levels have been for me incomparably more important than fragmentary conversations with celebrities' (*MDR* 143).

Above all, he never forgot that every patient was unique, and that general rules, dogmatic ideas, and universal procedures should never be applied to him. 'Learn your theories,' he taught his students. 'Then, when the patient walks in through the door, forget them.' He was hostile to group therapy and to all mass-produced remedies. 'In dealing with individuals, only individual understanding will do.'

It will be seen that Jung's approach to a patient differed radically from that of the conventional psychiatrist, who applies the 'medical model' to all who consult him, focusing on the signs and symptoms of illness in order to establish 'what has gone wrong', make a diagnosis, and prescribe treatment, while always maintaining clinical distance and professional authority. Jung, on the other hand, approached the patient not from the standpoint of pathology but from an anticipation of health in an effort to establish 'what can go right'; his focus was on symbols and meanings rather than symptoms, discovering what archetypal needs had been frustrated and needed to be met, while relating to the patient through the personal intimacy and 'mutuality' of the analytic situation. The essential difference between the two approaches is that the psychiatrist sees the patient as a victim of illness, the Jungian as a candidate for individuation.

Treatment

The Jungian approach to treatment is, again, very different from conventional psychiatry. The psychiatrist is concerned to reduce suffering through the provision of medicine and support, whereas the Jungian encourages the patient to *participate* in his suffering so as to confront its meaning and mobilize the healing powers of the unconscious. To face the major issues of life can involve much pain but this is a valuable spur to self-examination, an incentive to 'wake up' to one's predicament and grow beyond it. Jung once remarked of a patient, 'Thank God he became neurotic!' For in this case, as in many others, the neurosis was a call to attend to what was lacking or problematic in his life and to embark on the journey of self-discovery and renewal.

To the psychiatrist, overwhelmed as he often is by large numbers of sick patients, mental illness is an enemy (on to which he projects his own sick shadow) to be fought and overcome, a 'devil' to be driven out. To the Jungian the illness is a symbolic communication from the unconscious indicating where the patient has got stuck in his efforts to meet the demands of the archetypal programme for life. In a psychiatric clinic the patient goes through the ritual of consultation, diagnosis, and treatment, colludes with the psychiatrist in becoming detached from his illness, and is encouraged to relinquish responsibility for his plight into the 'capable hands' of the doctor. The Jungian, on the other hand, treats the whole patient, encouraging him to accept full responsibility for his circumstances, and to understand his illness as an expression of his total life experience. He is taught to see his symptoms as arising from an unbalanced mode of existence, which is itself a result of thwarted archetypal intent. Treatment consists of helping him to recognize and find ways of correcting his archetypal frustration, abandoning his one-sidedness, and bringing about a new equilibrium between the opposing forces in his personality as a whole.

To achieve this it is not sufficient to confine himself to dealing with his conscious circumstances. It is essential to know the situation in the unconscious. Here the analysis of dreams and the analysis of the transference become indispensable. The psychiatric approach is quite different: the aim is not to open up the unconscious, or receive the messages it has to convey, but to suppress it, to silence it with drugs. The goal of psychiatry is first aid and 'rehabilitation'—to return the patient to the community. The possibility that a breakdown may be a crisis filled with existential meaning and an opportunity for growth is seldom considered.

In fairness to the psychiatric profession, however, it must be acknowledged that Jung's patients, once he had left the Burghölzli, were hardly the run-of-the-mill intake of psychiatric practice. Most of them were educated, well-off, and in the second half of life. A number of them were psychologically sophisticated in that they had already received some form of psychotherapy before consulting him, and a fair proportion of them had little that was psychiatrically wrong with them. 'About a third of my cases are not suffering from any clearly definable neurosis, but from the senselessness and aimlessness of their lives. I should not object if this were called the general neurosis of our age' (*CW* XVI, para. 83).

To what did he attribute the 'general neurosis of our age'? To a collective 'loss of soul': to a loss of contact with the great mythic and religious symbols of our culture, to the emergence of social institutions which alienate us from our archetypal nature. This is an extension of the view advanced by philosophers such as Diderot and Nietzsche, and later developed by Freud in *Civilization and Its Discontents*, that the benefits of civilization are bought at the cost of natural happiness. Jung believed that the more secular, materialistic, and compulsively extraverted our civilization became, the greater the unhappiness, 'senselessness and aimlessness' of our lives. What was the answer? Not 'a return to the Church', for his own experience had taught him that—unless it came as a gnostic revelation—organized religion meant spiritual death. Again as a result of his own experience, he felt that we had no other recourse than to abandon the exclusively extraverted quest for meaning in the outer world of material objects so typical of our culture and, instead, establish contact with the symbol-forming capacities latent within our own psychic nature. What was needed was hard psychological work to open our minds to the inner wealth of the unconscious in order to realize in actuality our own capacity for wholeness. In the process, meaning and purpose flood back into our lives.

Jung divided analysis into four stages, which inevitably overlap and certainly do not always proceed in a regular order. These are:

(i) *Confession*: this is the stage of initial catharsis when one shares with the analyst the secrets one has been carrying. This is usually associated with feelings of intense relief, of shedding a burden, of discharging a load of poison. Guilty feelings are reduced, as are feelings of being isolated, inferior, and beyond the pale. The integration of the shadow begins.

(ii) *Elucidation*: this is roughly equivalent to Freudian 'interpretive' analysis. Symptoms and transference phenomena are examined and areas of failed development located. Radical transformations are rare at this stage; but serious work with the unconscious has started.

(iii) *Education*: the insights gained in stages (i) and (ii) are now ploughed into life. One begins to experience oneself differently and to explore new modes of existing. This usually goes along with an improved adaptation to the demands of society.

(iv) *Transformation*: work with the unconscious brings one face to face with the shadow, the anima or animus, and other archetypal components which are activated, as a natural homeostatic compensation, for one's previously narrow, neurotic, or one-sided development. At this stage, the transcendent function of symbols comes into its own. The individuation quest is now under way and is associated with coming to 'selfhood', a state reaching beyond mere 'normality' or 'social adaptation' to a full affirmation and acceptance of oneself as a whole entity in one's own right.

Jung elucidated the analytic process in the light of his alchemical studies. He acknowledged that, like alchemy, analysis is not a science but an art, an *ars spagyrica*—a spagyric art. 'Spagyric' is derived from two Greek words, *span* meaning to rend, to separate, to stretch out (i.e. to analyse) and *ageirein*, to collect together or assemble (i.e. to synthesize). The alchemical slogan *solve et coagula* (dissolve and coagulate) precisely expresses these two steps: 'The alchemist saw the essence of his art in separation and analysis on the one hand and synthesis and consolidation on the other' (Foreword to *CW* XIV). The analytic phase corresponds to the reductive method of Freud and the first two stages of Jungian analysis, and the second, synthetic phase to the last two stages.

Whether or not an analysis succeeds in its objectives depends on the raw materials (the alchemical *prima materia*) which patient and analyst bring with them to the analytical situation (the retort; the *vas*) and the transformation that occurs through their interaction. The first requirement is that both accept full responsibility for themselves and their own contributions to the relationship. 'The doctor must emerge from his anonymity and give an account of himself, just as he expects his patients to do' (*CW* XVI, para. 23).

Initially, most patients find it hard to accept responsibility for themselves and for their illness, preferring to hold others responsible and to adopt a passive or dependent attitude to the analyst. But this has to change if the analysis is ever to progress beyond the second stage: 'The real therapy only begins when the patient sees that it is no longer father and mother who are standing in his way, but himself . . .' (*CW* VII, para. 88).

Persuading the patient to be responsible for his illness can require great tact, otherwise he may adopt a moral attitude of self-condemnation because of it. He needs to understand that the illness is not his 'fault' but that he alone can discover its meaning and find a cure. The objective is to encourage a creative relationship both to the illness and to the personality as a whole and not to engender guilt or remorse.

The techniques of Jungian analysis—the two chairs, the dialectical mutuality between equals, the relatively frequent breaks and progressive reduction in the number of sessions, the personal work on dreams and 'active imagination' outside the analytic situation—are all designed to heighten this sense of responsibility in the patient for his own process of growth.

Jung banished the couch from the consulting room for this reason. Because it made the patient passive and dependent it positively encouraged a Freudian regression to the infantile complexes and hindered the onset of the collaborative, prospective adventure that Jung conceived analysis to be. Although Jung took full account of what his patient had been in the past, he was far more interested in what the patient was in the process of *becoming* in the present. Sitting face to face on similar chairs also made it easier for both therapist and patient to experience themselves as colleagues working on a shared task and to test the reality of whatever projections they might make on one another.

With regard to the frequency of sessions, Jung was critical of the Freudian practice of seeing patients intensively over long periods of time.

The psychoanalyst thinks he must see his patient for an hour a day for months on end; I manage in difficult cases with three or four sittings a week. As a rule I content myself with two, and once the patient has got going, he is reduced to one. In the interim he has to work at himself, but under my control. I provide him with the necessary psychological knowledge to free himself from my medical authority as speedily as possible. In addition, I break off the treatment every ten weeks or so, in order to throw him back on his normal milieu. . . . In such a procedure time can take effect as a healing factor, without the patient's having to pay for the doctor's time. With proper direction most people become capable after a while of making their contribution—however modest at first—to the common work. In my experience the absolute period of cure is not shortened by too many sittings. (*CW* XVI, para. 43)

Jung's assertion that the time needed for an analysis is not shortened by maintaining a high number of weekly sessions is supported by research which has failed to demonstrate that five sessions produces results superior to what can be achieved by one or two sessions a week. There are analysts, however, especially Freudians, and also some post-Jungians of the 'Developmental' school, who maintain as an article of faith that *analysis* means four or five sessions a week, 'otherwise it is not analysis'. Jung would have scorned this idea. In any case, the analytic process cannot be hurried. Inevitably the 'spagyric art' requires time for its goals to be accomplished.

Another aspect of Jung's practice which most analysts have chosen to ignore (often out of financial necessity) is his advice to break off the analysis every ten weeks to throw the patient back into life, to discourage reliance on the analyst, and to encourage reliance on the Self. This way the patient does not live to analyse, but analyses to live. This can be of immense benefit to analysts as well as to patients, for it helps prevent the exhaustion that can so easily afflict hard-working therapists and to ensure against their work becoming 'routine' or lifeless. A regular break from clinical responsibilities can enable analysts to follow other pursuits, such as studying, writing, lecturing, painting, pottery, travel, and sport, so that they can recharge their creative energies and strengthen their immunity to those forms of psychic contagion and 'burn out' that are common among therapists, social workers, and psychiatrists.

It must be acknowledged, however, that some patients find it impossible to work this way, especially those who, as a result of defective parenting in childhood, suffer from 'borderline' or 'narcissistic' personality disorders, or from what Bowlby called 'anxious attachment'. Such patients need time to establish with their analyst a working relationship through which they can begin to conceive of themselves as capable of sustaining a lasting bond of intimacy and trust. Only when this has been achieved can they begin to benefit from the kind of imaginative work with the unconscious that Jungians regard as the crux of analysis. Apart from these and some other exceptions, the classical Jungian approach can be applied with benefit to patients with widely differing kinds of personal difficulties and neurotic disorders.

To Jung, work with the unconscious was his way of life, and its objective was quite simply to *be* in the soul (*esse in anima*). This meant being constantly alive to the creative originality of the psyche. 'Being that has soul is living being. Soul is the living thing in man, that which lives of itself and causes life . . .' (*CW* IX. i, para. 59). Things come alive and are touched with soul when they come under the influence of the imagination. 'The psyche creates reality everyday, the only expression I can use for this activity is fantasy' (*CW* VI, para. 78).

The secret, both of analysis and of life, is to participate in this fantasy, both in our sleeping and our waking lives. 'In sleep fantasy takes the form of dreams. But in waking life, too, we continue to dream below the threshold of consciousness' (*CW* XVI, para. 125). The soul accompanies us as a constant companion, but we generally ignore its utterances because we fail to hear them. This can be rectified not only by attending to our dreams but also through the practice of *active imagination*. This is a technique for granting the psyche freedom and time to express itself spontaneously, without the usual interference of the ego. It is 'the art of letting things happen' that he observed in Hélène Preiswerk during her seances and in himself during his confrontation with the unconscious. 'The art of letting things happen, action through non-action, letting go of oneself, as taught by Meister Eckhart, became for me the key opening the door to the way. We must be able to let things happen in the psyche' (Foreword, *The Secret of the Golden Flower*, Richard Wilhelm, Routledge & Kegan Paul, 1962, 93).

Active imagination requires a state of reverie, half-way between sleep and waking. It is like beginning to fall asleep but stopping short before consciousness is lost, and then remaining in that condition, and observing what occurs. It is important to record what has been experienced, so as to make it lastingly available to consciousness: it can be written down, painted, modelled in clay, or even danced or acted.

To begin with one is usually a mere spectator, but if one is to experience the *reality* of the psyche and truly submit to its transformative power then one must enter the fantasy and become a committed participant in the drama:

You yourself must enter into the process with your personal reactions, just as if you are one of the fantasy figures, or rather, as if the drama being enacted before your eyes were real. It is a psychic fact that this fantasy is happening, and it is as real as you—as a psychic entity—are real. If this crucial operation is not carried out, all the changes are left in the flow of images, and you yourself remain unchanged. (*CW* IV, para. 753)

Again, as a result of his own experience, Jung was particularly keen that his patients should paint their psychic images.

The patient can make himself creatively independent through this method, if I may call it such. He is no longer dependent on his dreams or on his doctor's knowledge; instead, *by painting himself he gives shape to himself.* For what he paints are active fantasies. . . . It is himself in a new and hitherto alien sense, for his ego now appears as the object of that which works within him. (*CW* XVI, para. 106)

Through learning to work on his own dreams and developing the knack of active imagination, the patient increasingly assumes responsibility for his life and for his own individuation.

Hence the interval between consultations does not go unused. In this way one saves oneself and the patient a good deal of time, which is so much money to him; and at the same time he learns to stand on his own feet instead of clinging to the doctor. The work done by the patient through the progressive assimilation of unconscious contents leads ultimately to the integration of his personality and hence to the removal of the neurotic dissociation. (*CW* XVI, paras. 26, 27)

The therapist

Many people, both medically qualified and lay persons, came to Jung saying that they wished to become analysts. He describes one of these applicants in his autobiography: he was a doctor, with an impeccable background, who came with the best recommendations. When he declared his intention of training as an analyst, Jung said him:

'Do you know what that means? It means that you must first learn to know yourself. You yourself are the instrument. If you are not right how can the patient be made right? If you are not convinced, how can you convince him? You must yourself be the real stuff. If you are not, God help you! Then you will lead your patients astray. Therefore you must first accept an analysis of yourself.' (*MDR* 134)

As it happened, Jung turned this man down after listening to his first dream: it revealed a latent psychosis. But his remarks demonstrate the emphasis he placed on the therapist fully undergoing the process which he intended to supervise in others. 'An ancient adept has said: "If the wrong man uses the right means, the right means work in the wrong way." This Chinese saying, unfortunately, only too true, stands in sharp contrast to our belief in the "right" method irrespective of the man who applies it. In reality, everything depends on the man and little or nothing on the method' (*CW* XIII, para. 4).

Not only is it necessary for the analyst to be analysed during his training, but he must continue to work on himself throughout his professional life.

The analyst must go on learning endlessly ... We could say, without too much exaggeration, that a good half of every treatment that probes at all deeply consists in the doctor's examining himself, for only what he can put right in himself can he hope to put right in the patient. It is no loss, either, if he feels that the patient is hitting him: or even scoring off him: it is his own hurt that gives the measure of his power to heal. This, and nothing else, is the meaning of the Greek myth of the wounded physician. (*CW* XVI, para. 239)

Self-analysis is necessary because of Jung's conception of what the analytic relationship entails, namely, a commitment on the part of the analyst that is at least as great as that of the patient. At the unconscious level both doctor and patient are participating in what the alchemists termed a *coniunctio*: like two chemical substances, they are drawn together in the analytic situation by *affinity*, and their interaction produces change. 'When two chemical substances combine, both are altered. This is precisely what happens in the transference' (*CW* XVI, para. 358).

The term 'transference' was first introduced by Freud to describe the unconscious process by which a patient attributes to the analyst feelings and attitudes that were, in fact, possessed by significant people in his past. This gives rise to the so-called *transference relationship*, which has to be distinguished from the *analytical relationship* or the *therapeutic alliance*, which refers to the total relationship between the analyst and patient as actual people.

Jung greatly extended the Freudian view of the transference, for he understood that the doctor–patient relationship is an archetypal relationship which has been with us since the beginning of time. In the course of an analysis archetypal images are stirred up which, when projected on to the person of the analyst, can confer upon him great therapeutic (or destructive) power. In Jung's own experience such archetypal figures as the magician, shaman, witch-doctor, and wise old man were commonly projected. Secondly, and most importantly from the point of view of therapeutic outcome, the analyst can receive the projection of previously unfulfilled archetypal needs. For example, he may become the powerful father figure that a patient lacked in childhood, and this was clearly a crucial component of Jung's own transference on to the person of Freud. Finally, unconscious activity in the patient causes reciprocal activity in the unconscious of the analyst, with the result that the bond between them is transformed into something much more profound than the conventional doctor–patient relationship. It is this aspect of the transference that makes it essential that the therapist should be thoroughly analysed and remain aware of his 'personal equation'. It then becomes possible for the analyst to recognize what is unconsciously projected on to his patient (the so-called *counter-transference*) and to use this constructively in the therapeutic relationship instead of allowing it to become disruptive.

Moreover, in contrast to analysts of other schools, Jung laid stress on the vital importance of *feeling*—not only the patient's feeling for the analyst but also the analyst's feeling for the patient. Feeling provides an invaluable catalyst. It has to be present in the ego's relationship with the unconscious no less than in the analytic relationship itself. This is particularly true when patient and analyst are both men or both women, success depending on each being in a feeling relationship with the other's unconscious. Some over-rational patients 'try to understand with their brains only . . . And when they have understood, they think they have done their full share of realization. That they should also have a *feeling relationship* to the contents of the unconscious seems strange to them or even ridiculous' (*CW* XVI, para. 489). Yet unless feeling is present no growth or transformation will occur.

Thus, in any thorough analysis, the personalities of both doctor and patient are fully engaged. In advancing this deeply committed view of the analytic relationship, Jung was fulfilling the vision of his life's work when, as a medical student, he read Krafft-Ebing's words that mental illnesses are 'diseases of the personality' and that to treat them the doctor must stand 'behind the objectivity of his experiences' and respond 'with the totality of his being'.

7   Jung's alleged anti-Semitism

I began by declaring Jung to be a man of paradox in that he followed a uniquely individual path towards discovery of the universal human being within himself. So true was he to his own 'little light' that many dismissed him as a crank and made little effort to penetrate his prose or make sense of his ideas. A number of those who did try to understand him got hold of the wrong end of the stick and, often unfairly, used it to beat him with. We can understand this in terms of Jung's psychological type. As an introverted thinking-intuitive type he had an extraverted feeling-sensation shadow. This means that he was capable of brilliant intellectual formulations and profound psychological insights, but it follows that both his feeling-based judgements and his relation to outer conditions could be defective. It is not uncommon for such types to feel impelled to state their vision of the truth boldly and uncompromisingly in circumstances where it would be more tactful and more politic to keep silent. Inevitably this earns them enemies as well as friends. Jung was aware of this drawback.

I have offended many people, for as soon as I saw that they did not understand me, that was the end of the matter so far as I was concerned: I had to move on. I had no patience with people—apart from my patients. I had to obey an inner law which was imposed on me and left me no freedom of choice. Of course, I did not always obey it. How can anyone live without inconsistency?   (*MDR* 328)

This can be construed as both a strength and a weakness. It enabled him to make discoveries and frame hypotheses that no one else would have dared to discover or propose at the time, thus enabling him to compensate for the anti-psychic, pro-environmentalist biases of behaviourism, for the reductive biases of Freudian psychology, and for the materialistic biases of our culture. On the other hand, it meant that some of his ideas provoked hostile opposition, while others were greeted with incomprehension or indifference. It also meant that he laid himself open to seriously damaging charges, such as the accusation that he was a racist.

113

This is not the place for a detailed examination of this accusation, but since it is repeated from time to time, and argued that all Jung's ideas should be dismissed on account of it, the reader has a right to know the substance of the allegation as well as Jung's side of the story.

Jung's accusers maintain that in the years following Hilter's accession to power in 1933 Jung behaved in such a way as to demonstrate that he was both an anti-Semite and a Nazi sympathizer. They substantiate this allegation on the basis of two pieces of evidence: (1) that he published articles arguing that there were differences between Jewish and Aryan psychology, and (2) that he became President of the (predominantly German) Medical Society of Psychotherapy in 1933, and turned it into an International Society of which he remained President until 1939—years after the German Society had officially 'conformed' (*gleichgeschaltet*) to Nazi ideology.

Jung did not dispute the truth of these statements but strenuously denied that he was either a Nazi or a racist. How then did he justify his behaviour? In the first place, the articles were published in a professional journal for psychotherapists, the *Zentralblatt für Psychotherapie*, many of whose readers were themselves Jews. In the early 1930s the Jewish–Aryan issue was, to put it mildly, much to the fore in peoples' minds. In Jung's view, the problem was largely one of shadow projection, the Aryans projecting their shadow on to the Jews, and vice versa. What was needed was an attempt to make *real* psychological differences between the two groups conscious in the hope that this would reduce shadow projection and make mutual acceptance easier.

When he was attacked for addressing these issues by a Swiss psychiatrist, Dr Gustav Bally, in the *Neue Züricher Zeitung* on 27 February 1934, Jung replied:

Admittedly I was incautious, so incautious as to do the very thing most open to misunderstanding at the present moment: *I have tabled the Jewish question*. This I did deliberately. My esteemed critic appears to have forgotten that the first rule of psychotherapy is to talk in the greatest detail about all the things that are the most ticklish and dangerous, and the most misunderstood. (*CW* X, para. 1024; italics added)

In this and other articles he argued that the difference between Freud's approach and his own had much to do with Freud's Jewish background and his own Christian upbringing:

I suggested years ago that every psychological theory should be criticized in the first instance as a subjective confession . . . This subjective premise is identical with our psychic idiosyncrasy. Idiosyncrasy is conditioned (1) by the individual, (2) by the family, (3) by the nation, race, climate, locality, and history . . . I am proud of my subjective premises, I love the Swiss earth in them, I am grateful to my theological forebears for having passed on to me the Christian premise . . .

Freud's Jewish psychology is similarly conditioned by the history of the Jewish people.

May it not be asked wherein lie the peculiar differences between an essentially Jewish and essentially Christian outlook . . . ? Are we really to believe that a tribe which has wandered through history for several thousand years as 'God's chosen people' was not put up to such an idea by some quite special psychological peculiarity? If no differences exist, how do we recognize Jews at all?

All branches of humanity originate from one stem, but what is a stem without separate branches? 'Why this ridiculous touchiness when anybody dares to say anything about the psychological difference between Jews and Christians? Every child knows that differences exist' (*CW* X, para. 1029).

Jung ends by denying that he has raised this issue out of sympathy for the Nazi position. He is merely repeating views he has held since 1913. However, 'It is, I frankly admit, a highly unfortunate and disconcerting coincidence that my scientific programme should, without any assistance of mine and against my express wish, have been linked up with a political manifesto.' (*CW* X, para. 1034)

With regard to the second accusation, that his Presidency of the Medical Society for Psychotherapy coincided with the first six years of Hitler's dictatorship, Jung's defence is that he accepted the Presidency specifically in order to protect the Society's Jewish members. The facts are as follows: the previous President of the Society, Professor Ernst Kretschmer, resigned when Hitler came to power in 1933, presumably because the *Gleichgeschaltung* (literally, 'bringing into step') of the Society was imminent. Jung, who was then Honorary Vice-President, agreed to take his place at the request of its leading members, but he made it conditional on there being radical amendments to the statutes turning the Society into an *international* organization.

This was done, with the result that the old Germany Society now became the *International General Medical Society for Psychotherapy*, made up of a number of different national sections, including Dutch, Danish, Swedish, and Swiss as well as German. The latter (the *Deutsche allgemeine ärtzliche Gesellschaft für Psychotherapie*) was established and 'conformed' in Berlin in September 1933 under the Presidency of the psychiatrist Professor M. H. Göring, cousin of the Reichsmarshall. One of Jung's first official acts as President of the International Society, at a Congress at Bad Nauheim in May 1934, was to stipulate that all German Jewish doctors who had been excluded from their 'conformed' national Society were now entitled to become individual members of the International Society, thus preserving equal social and professional rights. Moreover, at the end of the Congress, Jung issued a circular letter to all members firmly stating the principle that 'The International Society is neutral as to politics and creed'.

These actions hardly point to anti-Semitic or Fascist sympathies on Jung's part. How is it, then, that these charges have a tendency to be repeated? One reason involves an apparently damning piece of evidence which Jung explained, but not to everyone's satisfaction. It arises out of his editorship of the *Zentralblatt für Psychotherapie* and his responsibility for what appeared in it. The *Zentralblatt* was published in Germany, as it had been since the foundation of the original Society. When it became the organ of the International Society, it was edited from Zürich by Jung. In the autumn of 1933, Professor Göring announced his intention of publishing a special supplement to the *Zentralblatt* for members of the German Society, obliging them to abide by the ideology of National Socialism. Jung was powerless to do anything about this because it was an exclusively German matter. However, when the December issue of the *Zentralblatt* appeared, Jung was appalled to discover that the publisher had included Göring's manifesto in the edition intended for international circulation which bore Jung's name as editor. In his 'Rejoinder to Dr Bally' Jung states this was done without his knowledge or approval. His accusers have declined to believe him. However, he publicly declared his innocence in 1934 (not after the war as some have maintained) and, if he was lying, there would have been no shortage of people able to expose him. Moreover, letters have come to light confirming Jung's story. For example, he wrote in March 1934 to Dr Olaf Brüel, a Danish co-founder of the International Society, saying that Göring's manifesto had appeared against Jung's 'express demand' that it should appear in a special issue 'signed by Göring and not by me'. Jung also wrote to the secretary of the Society, Walter Cimbal, protesting against what had occurred, and adding an urgent request that all future issues of the *Zentralblatt* intended for international circulation should be 'unpolitical in every respect'.

Another difficulty for Jung arises from the language used by him in his articles on Aryan and Jewish differences and from the fact that he perceives Freud's attribution of a 'negative value' to the unconscious as a threat to our culture, because it could help to release the destructive forces accumulating in the Aryan psyche.

As a member of a race with a three-thousand-year-old civilization, the Jew, like the cultured Chinese, has a wider area of psychological consciousness than we. Consequently it is *in general* less dangerous for the Jew to put a negative value on his unconscious. The 'Aryan' unconscious, on the other hand, contains explosive forces and seeds of a future yet to be born, and these may not be devalued as nursery romanticism without psychic danger. The still youthful Germanic peoples are fully capable of creating new cultural forms that still lie dormant in the darkness of the unconscious of every individual—seeds bursting with energy and capable of mighty expansion. The Jew, who is something of a nomad, has never yet created a cultural form of his own and as far as we can see never will, since all his instincts and talents require a more or less civilized nation to act as host for their development. (*CW* X, para. 353)

Jung goes on to suggest that the Aryan unconscious has a 'higher potential' than the Jewish because it has 'a youthfulness not yet fully weaned from barbarism', as is evidenced by 'the formidable phenomenon of National Socialism, on which the whole world gazes with astonishment' (*CW* X, para. 354).

The expression of such sentiments as these, in a journal published in Nazi Germany, it has been suggested, puts Jung in the same conceptual frame as Adolf Hitler. This extremely hostile judgement takes little account of the social attitudes prevailing in all European countries at the time. The culture in which Jung grew up was inherently anti-Semitic. By our contemporary standards it was a racist society. Even the best-educated Europeans believed that blacks were inferior and that Jews were a problem. Both propositions were accepted by the majority as self-evident, hard though this is to believe for people born after 1945—that fateful year when a tidal wave of horror engulfed the European spirit and transformed our understanding of what it can mean to belong to a minority group.

By the standards of the first four decades of this century Jung was no racist. On the contrary, he was humane, broad-minded, and liberal. Far from being typical of the Swiss bourgeois his enemies have described, his ideas were highly innovative and far ahead of his time. For example, he advocated the decriminalization of homosexuality soon after the turn of the century, seeing it as both morally acceptable and a useful form of birth control; he risked his professional reputation by joining Freud when the latter was widely execrated for his views on infantile sexuality; and he advanced the deeply subversive idea that inside every man was an intact female personality, and a male personality inside every woman, which ought to be made conscious, integrated, and lived. As he wrote to Freud towards the end of their friendship, 'I should never have joined you in the first place had not heresy run in my blood' (*The Freud/Jung Letters*, 491, March, 1912).

It may be said of Jung that he was both tactless and politically inept to address the question of Jewish–Gentile relations in the way that he did, but Freud has never been attacked for doing the same thing. After their friendship had ended, Freud wrote to Sandor Ferenczi acknowledging that he had failed to unite 'Jews and goyim in the service of psychoanalysis', adding that 'They separate themselves like oil and water'. In another letter to Ferenczi he wrote, 'Certainly there are great differences between the Jewish and the Aryan spirit. We can observe that every day. Hence there would assuredly be here and there differences in outlook on life and art. But there should not be such a thing as Aryan or Jewish science.' This would be true enough of psychoanalysis and analytical psychology if they were indeed sciences (in the sense of physics or chemistry) but since they are not sciences but hermeneutic ('interpretive') disciplines, Jung's view of them both as 'subjective confessions', coloured by the personalities and cultures of their originators, is closer to the mark.

Jung has been much criticized for his argument (quoted above) that Jews needed a 'host' nation in which to develop their instincts and talents, since this could imply that Jews were, as the Nazis obsessively maintained, 'parasites'. Yet Freud is never criticized for using the same terminology. In *Moses and Monotheism*, published in 1938, Freud discusses ways in which Jews differ from non-Jews, acknowledging 'the fact that in some respects they are different from their "host" nations. . . . There is no doubt that they have a particularly high opinion of themselves, that they regard themselves as more distinguished, of higher standard, as superior to other peoples. . . . We know the reason for this behaviour and what their secret treasure is. They really regard themselves as God's chosen people . . .' Freud is allowed to make such statements because he was a Jew. Jung is not because he was a Gentile.

If the charge against Jung of anti-Semitism is unfair, where did it originate? Jung was in no doubt: 'This suspicion emanated from Freud' (*CW* X, para. 166). There is reason to believe this is true. A letter exists which Freud wrote to Jung's first psychoanalytic patient, a Russian Jewess called Sabina Spielrein. It was written in 1913 shortly after she gave birth to a son and just before the psychoanalytic conference in Munich: 'I am, as you know, cured of the last shred of my predilection for the Aryan cause, and would like to take it that if the child turns out to be a boy he will develop into a stalwart Zionist. . . . I shall not present my compliments to Jung in Munich, as you know perfectly well. . . . We are and remain Jews. The others will only exploit us and will never understand or appreciate us.' Freud's biographer, Ernest Jones, was aware of how quick Freud and his Viennese circle were to diagnose anti-Semitism in their opponents. He says he became aware, somewhat to his astonishment, 'of how extraordinarily suspicious Jews could be of the faintest sign of anti-semitism and of how many remarks or actions could be interpreted in that sense'. Freud was no exception. 'He had the common Jewish sensitiveness to the slightest hint of anti-Semitism and he made very few friends who were not Jews.'

As Jung well knew, bitter feelings were engendered in the Freudian camp by his 'defection' and many nefarious motives were

Jung

attributed to him to account for his behaviour: unfortunately, these prejudices have persisted in some Freudian and Jewish circles to the present day.

The injustice of the charges against Jung has been condemned by the Jews who knew him best. Gerhard Adler, James and Hilda Kirsch, Rivkah Kluger, Sigmund Hurwitz, and Jung's secretary, Aniela Jaffé, have all come staunchly to his defence, describing the generous assistance he gave to Jewish colleagues and their families who were fleeing from Nazi persecution and denying that he ever displayed anti-Semitic or pro-Nazi feelings. As long as he remained President of the International Society for Psychotherapy, Jung continued to uphold the right of Jews to participate fully in the Society's affairs, despite what he called in 1938 'the political psychosis of the day'. He resigned only when the psychosis spilled over into the Second World War. Throughout the war, even in the darkest days when it looked as if the Nazis would triumph, Jung was a fervent supporter of the allied cause, as his own letters and many independent witnesses testify.

At the end of the war, he had a significant interview with Leo Baeck, an eminent rabbi and professor of religion, who had survived three years in Theresienstadt concentration camp. On his arrival in Zürich in 1946, Baeck declined an invitation from Jung, so Jung went to see him at his hotel. They talked for two hours, during which Baeck reproached him with all the accusations that he had heard against him. Jung answered all these to Baeck's satisfaction and they parted on good terms.

In the course of their discussion, Jung admitted that he had 'slipped up' in his initial assessment of the National Socialist phenomenon. What did he mean by this? Like everyone else at the time, he had been impressed by Hitler's meteoric rise to power and recognized that the dictator must have tapped some extraordinary energy in the Teutonic unconscious. However, by the end of 1934, he was as aware as any shrewd observer that this energy was being channelled in evil and pathological directions. The truth is that if National Socialism interested him, it was as a *psychological* rather than a political phenomenon: it was an example of archetypes functioning at a suprapersonal level; it accorded with his observation that repressed archetypal components tend to erupt from the unconscious in primitive and destructive ways.

With extraordinary prescience, Jung actually predicted the Nazi eruption in a paper published as early as 1918:

Christianity split the Germanic barbarian into an upper and a lower half, and enabled him, by repressing the dark side, to domesticate the brighter half and fit it for civilization. But the lower, darker half still awaits redemption and a second spell of domestication. Until then, it will remain associated with the vestiges of the prehistoric age, with the collective unconscious, which is subject to a peculiar and ever-increasing activation. As the Christian view of the world loses its authority, the more menacingly will the 'blond beast' be heard prowling about in its underground prison, ready at any moment to burst out with devastating consequences. (*CW* X, para. 17)

Christianity, combined with the disciplined, hierarchical structure of German society, had repressed the Wotanic elements in the Teutonic unconscious—the passionate, irrational god of storm and frenzy, the god of war whose violent spirit takes possession of the hearts of men and drives them berserk with the lust for blood and destruction. These terrible archetypal vestiges were now on the move. Writing in 1936, he ventured 'the heretical suggestion that the unfathomable depths of Wotan's character explain more of National Socialism' than rational explanations based on economic or political causes (*CW* X, para. 385).

German mythology is unique in that its gods are overthrown by the powers of darkness. The whole mythic drama ends in *Ragnorok* as Valhalla is consumed with flames, like the Third Reich in 1945. In 1936 Jung perceived Hitler to be in the grip of these previously repressed Wotanic elements: 'The impressive thing about the German phenomenon is that one man, who is obviously "possessed" has infected a whole nation to such an extent that everything is set in motion and has started rolling on its course towards perdition' (*CW* X, para. 388).

It is fair to conclude, therefore, that Jung was not a Nazi supporter or an anti-Semite, and one must sympathize with him when he wrote: 'It must be clear to anyone who has read any of my books that I never have been a Nazi sympathizer and I never have been anti-semitic, and no amount of misquotation, mistranslation, or rearrangement of what I have written can alter the record of my true point of view' (*C. G. Jung Speaking*, 193).

Jung was temperamentally incapable of being a Nazi. He was hostile to all mass movements because they negated the primary value of the individual psyche. He loathed 'isms' and distrusted dogma in whatever form it took. Like everyone else, he had a shadow and, growing up in the culture that he did, it would be surprising if there were no Fascist or anti-Semitic attitudes in it. But unlike many of his detractors, one suspects, Jung *worked* on his shadow: 'It is indeed no small matter to know one's own guilt and one's own evil, and there is certainly nothing to be gained by losing sight of one's shadow. When we are conscious of our guilt we are in a more favourable position—we can at least hope to change and improve ourselves' (*CW* X, para. 440). It was in this spirit that he confessed to Leo Baeck that he had 'slipped up'.

In recent years a number of Jungians have raked over the evidence in order to confront these issues as openly as possible, and the results of their deliberations have been published in *Lingering Shadows* (Boston: Shambhala, 1991). Some authors of this collection of essays interpret the available material as indicating that Jung indeed held anti-Semitic views, but theirs is a minority opinion among the Jungian community as a whole. Those who continue to press accusations against Jung (and they are mostly from outside this community) doubtless have reasons for their persistence. One possibility is that they have not worked sufficiently on their own repressed Fascist, anti-Semitic, or anti-Christian shadows, and enjoy the glow of self-righteousness that comes as they project them on to Jung.

8   The summing-up

Had Jung been a Nazi sympathizer would this provide grounds for rejecting analytical psychology *in toto*? Some insist that it would, apparently in the belief that a man's views should conform to contemporary notions of political correctness before serious attention can be granted to his work. Their contention could be justified were it proved that analytical psychology, so closely derived from the psychology of its founder, is imbued with a Fascist spirit. Fortunately, its emphasis on the primary importance of the individual psyche and the personal quest for wholeness, combined with its resistance to dogmatism, collectivism, and social conformity, places analytical psychology in an intellectual position as far removed from Fascism as it is possible to be.

Jung was hostile to all political movements that sought to augment the powers of the state, for they would deprive the individual of his right to become *authentic*—to be true to the law of his own being: 'To the extent that a man is untrue to the law of his own being and does not rise to personality, he has failed to realize his life's meaning' (*CW* XVII, para. 314). Those who toe the party line do not choose their own way but submerge their potential for wholeness in a relatively unconscious existence of collective conformity. The increasing dependence of the individual on the state which characterized the political developments of his time Jung regarded as anything but healthy: 'it means that the whole nation is by way of becoming a herd of sheep, constantly relying on a shepherd to drive them into good pastures. The shepherd's staff soon becomes a rod of iron, and the shepherds turn into wolves' (*CW* X, para. 413).

However, some, for whom Jung's alleged Fascism is not an issue, have found other reasons for rejecting his ideas, arguing that they are too distorted by the typical assumptions of a man born in his time (1875), place (Switzerland), and class (professional 'bourgeoisie') to possess universal validity. For example, the theory of individuation is criticized as being too evidently determined by Jung's introverted psychological type, his therapeutic approach as too focused on inner events and insufficiently concerned with personal relationships, and his spiritual orientation as too influenced by his religious background for his Psychology to have much relevance to the existential problems of people living in the world today.

There must be some truth in these criticisms: everyone, however brilliant, must be born somewhere, at some time, in some community, and must inevitably bear the limitations of that fate. The introverted, individualistic, and spiritual biases of Jungian Psychology are evident and undeniable. But what matters in one who grapples with the crucial issues of human existence is the extent to which he can acknowledge his parochial origins, and, through an effort of intellect and imagination, transcend them. This was, as it happens, one of Jung's most extraordinary—and most paradoxical—gifts: his ability to live *in* his time and, simultaneously, to step out of it, to share an affinity with people of all the times that have ever been. Everything he wrote was touched by this affinity; and it has been justly said of him that his ideas were too fundamental, in a sense, to be modern. Precisely because he was so introverted, imaginative, and in love with introspection, he could peer hard and long into the mirror of his inner Self, and the vision of humanity that he saw there is as penetrating, far-sighted, and comprehensive as any yet described.

Jung's gift for transcending the confines of his own consciousness began, as we have seen, in the fantasy games of his childhood. Perhaps the most significant of these was the game involving the stone in the vicarage garden at Klein-Hüningen (p. 4 above): 'Am I the one who is sitting on the stone, or am I the stone on which *he* is sitting?' This recurrent ritual can be understood as the pathological behaviour of an emotionally deprived child who, lacking 'basic trust', in the world of people, compensates for his social isolation by constructing an imaginary relationship with a stone. However, such a reductive interpretation, though valid as far as it goes, neglects the highly significant consequences of the game for the child and his adult career. In this dialogue with the stone the seeds of Jungian Psychology are already germinating—the principles of duality, opposition, and enantiodromia, the animating power of the imagination which, through projection, quickens the world with life and meaning, the inner dialectic of thesis, antithesis, and synthesis central to psychic balance and growth.

The stone was Jung's first intimate encounter with the unconscious: out of it came his fascination with the unknown and his
later understanding, confirmed on the Athai Plains, of the *religious*
function of the psyche, that it provides the means through which
creation becomes conscious of itself. By projecting his psyche into
the stone he gave the stone life, identity, consciousness, doing
what the alchemists did as they gazed into the *prima materia* in
their retorts. He came to see the imagination as the psychic
quicksilver out of which everything of value is created; for the
material world of objects is devoid of all meaning save that which
we grant it in the psyche.

Insights such as these exposed him to two further criticisms,
namely, that his Psychology was essentially egocentric and antisocial, and that it was also unscientific: Jung took insufficient
account of the social influences on personality development and
his therapeutic procedures were not designed to promote adjustment to the demands of society. There is some justice in these
criticisms, as I believe Jung recognized. But so deeply introverted
was he that he felt it was only through conscious realization of the
inner world that relationship to outer reality was achieved. 'Relationship to the Self is at once relationship to our fellow man, and
no one can be related to the latter until he is related to himself'
(*CW* XVI, para. 445). Individuation, he declared, has two principal
aspects: 'In the first place it is an internal and subjective process of
integration, and in the second it is an equally indispensable process
of objective relationship' (*CW* XVI, para. 448). 'You cannot
individuate on Everest,' he said (Hannah, *Jung: His Life and Work*,
290). Individuation does not shut one out from the world but
gathers the world to oneself (*CW* VIII, para. 432).

When he eventually discovered in himself the security that was
absent from his childhood environment, the 'inner certainty' this
gave him enabled him to go his own way, to stand up to Freud and
the academic psychologists, and, like William Blake, another introverted visionary, to live in *compensatory* relationship to his
Age. If Freud espoused the principles of causality and psychic
determinism, concentrated on the psychopathology of childhood,
and damned religion as an infantile desire for parental protection,
then Jung countered by adopting a teleological perspective, en-
dorsed the freedom of the will, extended the developmental process

beyond childhood to the whole span of life, proposed that illness is itself a form of growth, and saw religion as the fulfilment of a basic human need.

The academic psychologists also drove him into a compensatory position. For most of his life psychology in the universities was dominated by behaviourism, with its dogmatic insistence on rigorous investigation of quantifiable behavioural responses to outer stimuli, banning the psyche and introspective techniques from the psychology laboratory, and denying the influence of innate structures on behaviour. Jung, by contrast, stressed the importance of symbolic experience and inner events, insisted that the psyche and its study through introspection took precedence above all else, and claimed that innate propensities provided the basis of all psychological knowledge and experience.

His cultural role was no less compensatory. Western society, detached from its Judeo-Christian roots, was compulsively materialistic, spiritually impoverished, and technologically obsessed. Collectively we were perpetuating the mistake of the alchemists, projecting our spiritual aspirations into material things in the delusion that we were pursuing the highest value. This had encouraged us to treat each other as economic commodities and exploit the physical resources of the planet while neglecting, to our own detriment, the spiritual resources of the Self. The only remedy for our civilization's 'loss of soul' was a massive reinvestment in the inner life of the individual, so as to re-establish a personal connection with 'the mythic world in which we were once at home by right of birth' (*MDR* 237). Deprived of the symbolism of myth and religion, people were cut off from meaning, and society was doomed to die.

It was for statements such as these that the academics condemned him as 'unscientific'. Jung was unconcerned: 'I cannot experience myself as a scientific problem. Myth is more individual and expresses life more precisely than does science' (*MDR* 17). Not that he was a stranger to scientific method, as his early researches show. But he had to look *beyond* science: 'Science comes to a stop at the frontiers of logic, but nature does not: she thrives on ground as yet untrodden by theory' (*CW* XVI, para. 524). What he refused to tolerate was the prevalent fallacy of *scientism*—the denial of everything that is not susceptible to a scientific explanation. He preferred to give due weight to those irrational, acausal experiences which science declines to consider worthy of its attention. In this sense, he saw 'scientific' psychology as anti-life: 'the more the critical reason dominates, the more impoverished life becomes; but the more myth we are capable of making conscious, the more life we integrate. Overvalued reason has this in common with political absolutism: under its domination the individual is pauperized' (*MDR* 280).

Analytical psychology can make no claim, therefore, to be an experimental science, any more than psychoanalysis: it is best classified as a branch of *hermeneutics*—the art of interpretation in the service of meaning. 'Man', said Jung at the end of a famous BBC television interview, 'cannot stand a meaningless life.' Where does meaning come from? Jung's answer is *through an unequivocal affirmation of the Self*. Being passionately on the side of individuation, the Self seeks growth and development in our lives. Affirmation of the Self liberates its creative energies and brings certain knowledge that the best life is the life lived *sub specie aeternitatis*: 'The decisive question for a man is this: Is he related to something infinite or not?' (p. 28 above). This, the ultimate question for mankind, has given rise to all the myths and religions ever created, each one being a brave attempt on the part of some human group to relate to the infinite, the eternal. The quest for the cosmic connection, the experience of the Sacred and Holy, is a fundamental requirement of the Self. To deny it brings spiritual decay; to embrace it illuminates the soul with meaning. 'I can only gaze with wonder and awe at the depths and heights of our psychic nature. Its non-spatial universe conceals an untold abundance of images which have accumulated over millions of years of development.' It is comparable in magnificence to the starry heavens at night, 'for the only equivalent of the universe within is the universe without' (*CW* IV, para. 331).

This cosmic perspective gave him his reverence for the unconscious and the unknown, for the *numinosity* of symbols, for the magical power of the imagination and the reconciling genius of the transcendent function, for the meaning we attribute to everything about us, for the primacy of the individual psyche as the link between our own lives and the inscrutable intentions of the great universe itself. His emphasis on the priceless value of the individual, his insistence on the supremacy of *gnosis* (knowledge through experience, not through book-learning or belief), his openness to the irrational, the spontaneous, the synchronistic, his celebration of the richly creative purposes of life, his realization of individuation as the goal to which all other goals are subservient, his recognition of dreams and myths as speaking the timeless language of the soul—all were expressions of the cosmogonic inspiration that filled his life.

There can be no doubt that Jung was an odd and unusual man, but his extraordinary achievement would not have been possible had he been any other than as he was. He expressed his credo at many different times in different ways, but there is one passage that sums it up better than any other: 'Personality is the supreme realization of the innate idiosyncrasy of a living being. It is an act of high courage flung in the face of life, the absolute affirmation of all that constitutes the individual, the most successful adaptation to the universal conditions of existence coupled with the greatest possible freedom for self-determination' (*CW* XVII, para. 289).

Though aware that our species and our planet are in grave peril from our own unconsciousness, he remained cautiously optimistic to the end. He believed that nothing essential is ever lost because its matrix is ever present among us and can always be recovered by those 'who have learned the art of averting their eyes from the blinding light of current opinions and close their ears to the noise of ephemeral slogans'. In a letter to M. Serranno (14 September 1960) written during the last year of his life he quoted the consolation given by an old alchemist to his disciple: 'No matter how isolated you are and how lonely you feel, if you do your work truly and conscientiously, unknown friends will come and seek you.' And a Chinese adage: 'The right man sitting in his house and thinking the right thought will be heard a hundred miles distant.'

The conclusion of the same letter provides a fitting epitaph:

I tried to find the best truth and the clearest light I could attain to, and since I have reached my highest point and can't transcend any more, I am guarding my light and my treasure . . . It is most precious not only to me, but above all to the darkness of the creator, who needs Man to illuminate his creation. If God had foreseen his world, it would be a mere senseless machine and Man's existence a useless freak. My intellect can envisage the latter possibility, but the whole of my being says 'No' to it.

Further Reading

In the present text I have endeavoured to define all special terms where they are first introduced, but anyone in need of a glossary will find one at the end of *Memories, Dreams, Reflections*. In addition, Daryl Sharp's *C. G. Jung Lexicon* (Toronto: Inner City Books, 1991), an invaluable primer of terms and concepts, is available in paperback.

Jungian psychology is as much a state of mind as a system of theory and practice. Hence Jung's quip: 'Thank God I'm Jung and not a Jungian,' and his insistence that all analysts must be analysed. The successful outcome of any analysis, whatever the theoretical allegiance of the analyst, depends less on the use of textbook procedures than on the spirit with which these procedures are applied. The spirit that informs the practice of analytical psychology is unequivocally that of its founder. Works by this extraordinary, rich, and complex personality are listed below.

Works by Jung

The Collected Works of C. G. Jung, ed. Herbert Read, Michael Fordham, and Gerhard Adler (20 vols.; London: Routledge, 1953–78). Quotations in the present work are identified by volume and paragraph number (e.g. *CW* VIII, para. 788). Readers with access to *CW* may like to use the quotations as a starting-point for their own explorations. The huge index (vol. XX) is an extremely helpful means of orientation.

Memories, Dreams, Reflections (London: Routledge & Kegan Paul, 1963; cited as *MDR* in this book), one of the most remarkable memoirs to be published this century.

Man and his Symbols (London: Aldus Books in association with W. H. Allen, 1964).

The Tavistock Lectures (*Analytical Psychology: Its Theory and Practice*, London: Routledge & Kegan Paul, 1968).

C. G. Jung: Psychological Reflections: A New Anthology of his Writings 1905–1961, selected and ed. Jolande Jacobi (London: Routledge & Kegan Paul, 1971).

Further Reading

C. G. Jung Letters, selected and ed. Gerhard Adler in collaboration with Aniela Jaffé (2 vols.; London: Routledge & Kegan Paul, 1973, 1976).

The Freud/Jung Letters, ed. William McGuire (London: The Hogarth Press and Routledge & Kegan Paul, 1974).

C. G. Jung Speaking, ed. William McGuire and R. C. F. Hull (London: Thames & Hudson, 1978).

Selected Writings, intro. Anthony Storr (London: Fontana Pocket Readers, 1983), warmly recommended for those not brave enough to tackle the *Collected Works* directly.

In addition there are a number of seminars, recorded by his students, several of which have been published.

Books about Jung

Writing about Jung remains a precarious business because certain crucial documents (e.g. his diaries and some of his letters) are still not in the public domain, and a definitive biography has yet to be written. However, much of significance can be gleaned from the following:

Bennet, E. A., *Meetings with Jung* (London: Anchor Press, 1982).

Brome, Vincent, *Jung: Man and Myth* (London: Macmillan, 1978).

Hannah, Barbara, *Jung: His Life and Work* (London: Michael Joseph, 1977).

Hopcke, Robert H., *A Guided Tour of the Selected Works of C. G. Jung* (Boston: Shambhala, 1989).

Jaffé, Aniela, *From the Life and Work of C. G. Jung* (London: Hodder & Stoughton, 1971).

Stern, Paul J., *C. G. Jung—The Haunted Prophet* (New York: George Brazillier, 1976).

Stevens, Anthony, *On Jung* (London: Penguin, 1990), examines the development of Jung's ideas in the context of his life and in relation to the life cycle of humanity.

Storr, Anthony, *Jung* (London: Fontana/Collins, 1973; Routledge, 1991).

van der Post, Laurens, *Jung and the Story of our Time* (New York: Pantheon Books, 1975).

von Franz, Marie-Louise, *C. G. Jung: His Myth in our Time* (London: Hodder & Stoughton, 1975).

Wehr, Gerhard, *Jung: A Biography* (Boston: Shambhala, 1987).

Post-Jungian Revisions

Papadopoulos, Renos (ed.), *Carl Gustav Jung: Critical Assessments* (London: Routledge, 1992).

Samuels, Andrew, *Jung and the Post-Jungians* (London: Routledge & Kegan Paul, 1985).

The most important developments, in my view, have been the extension of archetypal theory into the realms of childhood development, feminine psychology, religious symbolism, social and political studies, mythology and cultural history. Some key works are cited below under each of these headings.

Childhood development

Fordham, Michael, *Children as Individuals* (London: Hodder & Stoughton, 1969).

Neumann, Erich, *The Child: Structure and Dynamics of the Nascent Personality* (London: Hodder & Stoughton, 1973).

Wickes, Frances G., *The Inner World of Childhood* (New York: Appleton-Century, 1966).

Feminine psychology

Harding, M. Esther, *The Way of All Women* (New York: Harper & Row, 1975).

Wehr, Demaris S., *Jung and Feminism: Liberating Archetypes* (London: Routledge, 1988).

Whitmont, Edward C., *Return of the Goddess: Femininity, Agression and the Modern Grail Quest* (London: Routledge & Kegan Paul, 1983).

Religious symbolism

Edinger, Edward, *Ego and Archetype: Individuation and the Religious Function of the Psyche* (New York: Putnam, 1972).

Hostie, Raymond, *Religion and the Psychology of Jung* (London: Sheed & Ward, 1957).

White, Victor, *God and the Unconscious* (London: Harvill, 1952).

Social and political studies

Bernstein, Jerome S., *Power and Politics* (Boston: Shambhala, 1989).

Further Reading

Odajnyk, Volodymyr Walter, *Jung and Politics* (New York: Harper & Row, 1976).

Progoff, Ira, *Jung's Psychology and its Social Meaning* (London: Routledge & Kegan Paul, 1953).

Mythology and cultural history

Campbell, Joseph, *The Hero with a Thousand Faces* (New York: Pantheon, 1949).

Eliade, Mircea, *Shamanism: Archaic Techniques of Ecstasy* (London: Routledge & Kegan Paul, 1964).

—— *Birth and Rebirth (or Rites and Symbols of Initiation)* (New York: Harper, 1975).

Henderson, Joseph L., *Thresholds of Initiation* (Middletown, Conn.: Wesleyan University Press, 1967).

Neumann, Erich, *The Origins and History of Consciousness* (New York: Pantheon Books, 1954).

—— *The Great Mother: An Analysis of the Archetype* (London: Routledge & Kegan Paul, 1955).

Books by the present author

Archetype: A Natural History of the Self (London: Routledge & Kegan Paul, 1982), a study of the biological foundations of Jungian theory, with particular reference to development in childhood and adolescence.

Withymead: A Jungian Community for the Healing Arts (London: Coventure/Element Books, 1986), a study of a therapeutic community.

The Roots of War: A Jungian Perspective (New York: Paragon House, 1989), on war.

Index

Index

complex (*cont.*):
  see also moral complex; Oedipus
    complex
coniunctio oppositorum 110
consciousness 30, 46, 55, 100
  see also ego-consciousness
cosmology 30, 127–8
counter-transference 111
creative illness 22–4
creativity 87, 107–9, 127
  and symptom formation 99–100
Critique of Pure Reason 7
cross 91–5
cryptomnesia 78
culture 51–2, 56–8, 118

Dante 23, 90
da Vinci, Leonardo 27
death and rebirth 57
deep structures 37
delusions 12, 14
denial 46, 49
depression 62, 74
development, *see* psychology
Discovery of the Unconscious, The
  22, 78
Divine Comedy, The 23
divorce 60, 62
Dorian Gray 48, 49
dragon 57
dreams 27, 47, 58, 81–95
  amplification of 87
  analysis of 103, 108
  compensatory function of 63, 84–5
  and individuation 63
  interpretation of 87–95
  'manifest' and 'latent' content of
    81–2
  as pure nature 83–4
  structure of 87–8
  see also Jung, Carl Gustav

Eckhart, Meister 7, 108
ego 34, 45, 46
  ego-consciousness 46, 84
  ego-defence mechanisms 46, 49
  ego-Self axis 34, 45
Ellenberger, Henri 22
enantiodromia 7

enemy 48
Eros 52
eternal ground 41
ethology 36–9, 63–4
evil 48
extraversion 23, 24, 37, 66–79
  and hysteria 98
Eysenck, Hans 79

fairy-tales 14, 58
fantasy 19, 20
father 52
  see archetype; complex; Jung, Carl
    Gustav
Faust 7
Fechner, Gustav Theodor 23
feeling 66–70
  and analysis 111–12
  feeling types 73–5
femininity 51–4
femme inspiratrice 17
Ferenczi, Sandor 118
Fliess, Wilhelm 16
Flournoy, Theodore 9
free association 23, 81–3
Freud, Anna 46
Freud, Sigmund 11–16, 22–3
  theory of dreams 81–2
  see also Jung, Carl Gustav,
    relations with
Freud/Jung Letters 17, 118
functional types 66–79

Galton, Sir Francis 11
gender 50–4, 57–8
Gilgamesh 23
gnosis 8, 127–8
Gnosticism 8, 91
God 6
Goethe, Johann Wolfgang von 2, 7,
  77
Göring, M. H. 116–17
Grail legend 89–95
growth 28–31, 44, 59, 62
Guggenbühl-Craig, Adolf 60
guilt 49, 50, 104

hallucinations 10, 12, 14
Hannah, Barbara 125

Index

Index

OXFORD

MORE OXFORD PAPERBACKS

This book is just one of nearly 1000 Oxford Paperbacks currently in print. If you would like details of other Oxford Paperbacks, including titles in the World's Classics, Oxford Reference, Oxford Books, OPUS, Past Masters, Oxford Authors, and Oxford Shakespeare series, please write to:

UK and Europe: Oxford Paperbacks Publicity Manager, Arts and Reference Publicity Department, Oxford University Press, Walton Street, Oxford OX2 6DP.

Customers in UK and Europe will find Oxford Paperbacks available in all good bookshops. But in case of difficulty please send orders to the Cash-with-Order Department, Oxford University Press Distribution Services, Saxon Way West, Corby, Northants NN18 9ES. Tel: 0536 741519; Fax: 0536 746337. Please send a cheque for the total cost of the books, plus £1.75 postage and packing for orders under £20; £2.75 for orders over £20. Customers outside the UK should add 10% of the cost of the books for postage and packing.

USA: Oxford Paperbacks Marketing Manager, Oxford University Press, Inc., 200 Madison Avenue, New York, N.Y. 10016.

Canada: Trade Department, Oxford University Press, 70 Wynford Drive, Don Mills, Ontario M3C 1J9.

Australia: Trade Marketing Manager, Oxford University Press, G.P.O. Box 2784Y, Melbourne 3001, Victoria.

South Africa: Oxford University Press, P.O. Box 1141, Cape Town 8000.

PHILOSOPHY IN OXFORD PAPERBACKS

Ranging from authoritative introductions in the Past Masters and OPUS series to in-depth studies of classical and modern thought, the Oxford Paperbacks' philosophy list is one of the most provocative and challenging available.

THE GREAT PHILOSOPHERS

Bryan Magee

Beginning with the death of Socrates in 399, and following the story through the centuries to recent figures such as Bertrand Russell and Wittgenstein, Bryan Magee and fifteen contemporary writers and philosophers provide an accessible and exciting introduction to Western philosophy and its greatest thinkers.

Bryan Magee in conversation with:

A. J. Ayer

Michael Ayers

Miles Burnyeat

Frederick Copleston

Hubert Dreyfus

Anthony Kenny

Sidney Morgenbesser

Martha Nussbaum

John Passmore

Anthony Quinton

John Searle

Peter Singer

J. P. Stern

Geoffrey Warnock

Bernard Williams

'Magee is to be congratulated . . . anyone who sees the programmes or reads the book will be left in no danger of believing philosophical thinking is unpractical and uninteresting.' Ronald Hayman, *Times Educational Supplement*

'one of the liveliest, fast-paced introductions to philosophy, ancient and modern that one could wish for' *Universe*

Also by Bryan Magee in Oxford Paperbacks:

Men of Ideas
Aspects of Wagner 2/e

OPUS

*General Editors: Walter Bodmer, Christopher Butler,
Robert Evans, John Skorupski*

A HISTORY OF WESTERN PHILOSOPHY

This series of OPUS books offers a comprehensive and
up-to-date survey of the history of philosophical ideas
from earliest times. Its aim is not only to set those ideas in
their immediate cultural context, but also to focus on
their value and relevance to twentieth-century thinking.

CLASSICAL THOUGHT

Terence Irwin

Spanning over a thousand years from Homer to Saint Augustine, *Classical Thought* encompasses a vast range of material, in
succinct style, while remaining clear and lucid even to those with
no philosophical or Classical background.

The major philosophers and philosophical schools are examined—the Presocratics, Socrates, Plato, Aristotle, Stoicism,
Epicureanism, Neoplatonism; but other important thinkers,
such as Greek tragedians, historians, medical writers, and early
Christian writers, are also discussed. The emphasis is naturally
on questions of philosophical interest (although the literary and
historical background to Classical philosophy is not ignored),
and again the scope is broad—ethics, the theory of knowledge,
philosophy of mind, philosophical theology. All this is presented
in a fully integrated, highly readable text which covers many of
the most important areas of ancient thought and in which stress
is laid on the variety and continuity of philosophical thinking
after Aristotle.

Also available in the History of Western Philosophy series:

The Rationalists   John Cottingham
Continental Philosophy since 1750   Robert C. Solomon
The Empiricists   R. S. Woolhouse

PAST MASTERS

General Editor: Keith Thomas

The *Past Masters* series offers students and general readers alike concise introductions to the lives and works of the world's greatest literary figures, composers, philosophers, religious leaders, scientists, and social and political thinkers.

'Put end to end, this series will constitute a noble encyclopaedia of the history of ideas.' Mary Warnock

HOBBES

Richard Tuck

Thomas Hobbes (1588–1679) was the first great English political philosopher, and his book *Leviathan* was one of the first truly modern works of philosophy. He has long had the reputation of being a pessimistic atheist, who saw human nature as inevitably evil, and who proposed a totalitarian state to subdue human failings. In this new study, Richard Tuck shows that while Hobbes may indeed have been an atheist, he was far from pessimistic about human nature, nor did he advocate totalitarianism. By locating him against the context of his age, Dr Tuck reveals Hobbs to have been passionately concerned with the refutation of scepticism in both science and ethics, and to have developed a theory of knowledge which rivalled that of Descartes in its importance for the formation of modern philosophy.

Also available in Past Masters:

PAST MASTERS

General Editor: Keith Thomas

Past Masters is a series of concise, lucid, and authoritative introductions to the thought of leading intellectual figures of the past whose ideas still affect the way we think today.

'One begins to wonder whether any intelligent person can afford not to possess the whole series.' *Expository Times*

FREUD

Anthony Storr

Sigmund Freud (1865–1939) revolutionized the way in which we think about ourselves. From its beginnings as a theory of neurosis, Freud developed psycho-analysis into a general psychology which became widely accepted as the predominant mode of discussing personality and interpersonal relationships.

From its inception, the psycho-analytic movement has always aroused controversy. Some have accepted Freud's views uncritically: others have dismissed psycho-analysis as unscientific without appreciating its positive contributions. Fifty years have passed since Freud's death, so it is now possible to assess his ideas objectively. Anthony Storr, psychotherapist and writer, takes a new, critical look at Freud's major theories and at Freud himself in a book which both specialists and newcomers to Freud's work will find refreshing.

Also available in Past Masters:

Homer   Jasper Griffin
Thomas More   Anthony Kenny
Galileo   Stillman Drake
Marx   Peter Singer

PAST MASTERS

General Editor: Keith Thomas

The people whose ideas have made history . . .

'One begins to wonder whether any intelligent person can afford not to possess the whole series.' *Expository Times*

JESUS

Humphrey Carpenter

Jesus wrote no books, but the influence of his life and teaching has been immeasurable. Humphrey Carpenter's account of Jesus is written from the standpoint of an historian coming fresh to the subject without religious preconceptions. And no previous knowledge of Jesus or the Bible on the reader's part is assumed.

How reliable are the Christian 'Gospels' as an account of what Jesus did or said? How different were his ideas from those of his contemporaries? What did Jesus think of himself? Humphrey Carpenter begins his answer to these questions with a survey and evaluation of the evidence on which our knowledge of Jesus is based. He then examines his teaching in some detail, and reveals the perhaps unexpected way in which his message can be said to be original. In conclusion he asks to what extent Jesus's teaching has been followed by the Christian Churches that have claimed to represent him since his death.

'Carpenter's *Jesus* is about as objective as possible, while giving every justifiable emphasis to the real and persistent forcefulness of the moral teaching of this charismatic personality.' Kathleen Nott, *The Times*

'an excellent, straightforward presentation of up-to-date scholarship' David L. Edwards, *Church Times*

Also available in Past Masters:

Muhammad   Michael Cook
Aquinas   Anthony Kenny
Cervantes   P. E. Russell
Clausewitz   Michael Howard

PAST MASTERS

General Editor: Keith Thomas

Past Masters is a series of concise and authoritative introductions to the life and works of men and women whose ideas still influence the way we think today.

'Put end to end, this series will constitute a noble encyclopaedia of the history of ideas.' Mary Warnock

SHAKESPEARE

Germaine Greer

'At the core of a coherent social structure as he viewed it lay marriage, which for Shakespeare is no mere comic convention but a crucial and complex ideal. He rejected the stereotype of the passive, sexless, unresponsive female and its inevitable concommitant, the misogynist conviction that all women were whores at heart. Instead he created a series of female characters who were both passionate and pure, who gave their hearts spontaneously into the keeping of the men they loved and remained true to the bargain in the face of tremendous odds.'

Germaine Greer's short book on Shakespeare brings a completely new eye to a subject about whom more has been written than on any other English figure. She is especially concerned with discovering why Shakespeare 'was and is a popular artist', who remains a central figure in English cultural life four centuries after his death.

'eminently trenchant and sensible . . . a genuine exploration in its own right' John Bayley, *Listener*

'the clearest and simplest explanation of Shakespeare's thought I have yet read' Auberon Waugh, *Daily Mail*

Also available in Past Masters: